ZEN OF THE FORGOTTEN MIND

SCOTT SHAW

BUDDHA ROSE PUBLICATIONS

Zen of the Forgotten Mind

www.scottshaw.com

Cover Photograph(s) by Scott Shaw

Rear Cover Photograph of Scott Shaw
by Hae Won Shin

First Edition 2026

ISBN 10: 1-949251-92-6
ISBN 13: 978-1-949251-92-0

Library of Congress Control Number: 2026939629

10 9 8 7 6 5 4 3 2 1
Printed in the United States of America

ZEN
OF THE
FORGOTTEN MIND

Introduction

Here it is, *The Scott Shaw Zen Blog 33.0,* originally presented on the *World Wide Web.* All of the writings presented in this book were written between November 2025 and April of 2026.

As was the case with the previously published volumes based upon *The Scott Shaw Zen Blog;* entitled: *Scribbles on the Restroom Wall, The Chronicles: Zen Ramblings from the Internet, Words in the Wind, Zen Mind Life Thoughts, The Zen of Life, Lies and Aberrant Reality, Apostrophe Zen, The Abstract Arsenal of Zen and the Psychology of Being, Zen and Again: The Metaphysical Philosophy of Psychology, Tempest in a Teapot and the Den of Zen, Buddha in the Looking Glass, Wo Ton' of the Blue Vision, Zen and the Psychology of the Spiritual Something, Pyrophoric Zen, Fragments of Paradox, Zen: Traversing the Entity of Non-Entity, Zen and the Ambient Echo: The Psychological Philosophy of Being, Paritical Zen and the Life Science of Becoming No Thing, Obscurist Occulto: Hiding from the Definition of Meaning, Principles of the Precepts, Left Turn at Reality Central, Zen and the Outside of the Inside, Garage Sale Zen, The Zen of Volume Destiny, Zen* and *Noted for Nothing, Zen and the Search for Suchness, Flash Point Zen, Zen and the Distinct Passageway to Nowhere, Zen and the Shadow of the Flower, Zen and the Last Call of the Illusion, Blank Space Zen, and Graveyard of the Buddhas* this volume is presented exactly as it was viewed on *scottshaw.com* with no rewriting, punctuation, or typo corrections. From this, we hope you will receive the original reading experience.

This volume of internet ramblings is presented with the date and time listed as to when each blog was originally posted. Also, the blogs in this volume are presented from last to first. With this, we hope to present a transcendence back through time as opposed to an evolving evolution. In addition, we left out the traditional *Table of Contents* in an attempt to leave this volume with a much more free-flowing reading experience.

Okay, there's the information and the definitions. Read on... We hope you enjoy it. And, be sure to stayed tuned for the ongoing *Scott Shaw Zen Blog @ scottshaw.com*

HAPPINESS POWERS ACTIVATE

02/Apr/2026 09:31 AM

How happy are you? Really, how happy are you?

How happy are you right now in this moment?

How happy are you in the greater, grand scheme of your life?

For most, happiness is something that happens quite randomly. Some situation occurs or some person does something and that emotion appears. With this and from this, happiness is embraced. But, for most of the time, the feeling of happiness is absent from the common emotions of a person's everyday life.

Think about this, how often do you feel happy?

Do you seek out people and situations that make you embrace this emotion? Or, is it vastly removed from your life as you are constrained by the stark reality of everyday existence?

Most people do not pursue a life based upon happiness. There are many other emotions that are seemingly far more of a driving factor for the existence of most. Emotions like anger, frustration, fear, jealousy, aggression are far more adrenaline inducing sensations.

But, ask yourself, isn't happiness a much better emotion to experience? Better than any emotion based in a negative mindset?

I remember when I was a young person, a teenager, waking the Spiritual Path. One of my teachers explained one day that a person could experience the sensation of love any time that they wished to. It did not need to be motivated by a person. You could simply find that feeling within yourself, consciously allow it to embrace you, and it would emanate from that internal place where it always exists, commonly

only instigated by that someone else, who you are, *"In love,"* with. Anyone can simply find that place that is love, within yourself, and call it up.

This is a technique I have used many times in my life. Both in association with someone else, and by myself.

I suggest that everyone give this technique a try. If not right now, perhaps when you are in a quiet place and of the right mind.

The thing being, if you can cause the emotion of love to rise within yourself, you can also do this with the emotion of happiness. We each know what happiness feels like. And thus, by knowing this feeling, we have the ability to call it up, at any time, within ourselves.

Again, if not right now, when you are in the right frame of mind, test this, allow yourself to simply feel happy. You know the experience, simply call it up within yourself.

Many people spend much of their life embracing a very unhappy state of mind. Do you?

The thing is, this does not have to be the definition of an individual's life. You can be happy.

We all go through the trial and tribulations of life. We each are dealt the hand of cards that life deals us. This being said, this does not mean that we must be dominated by all of that outside, uncontrollable, stimuli. We can be in control of ourselves and our emotions.

You can be happy. You can be happy no matter what. You simply must choose to be happy.

Whenever you feel the need—whenever you need to, simply allow happiness to arise within you. You have the power. You can be happy.

Trust me, following the pathway of happiness is far better than most other corridors of life.

WALK LIKE A NINJA
01/Apr/2026 07:36 AM

Have you ever noticed that some people are very loud? The stomp when they walk. They speak very loudly. They like to yell. They don't close cabinet drawers, they slam them. When they put dishes or pans away, they shove them in and around, making a lot of noise. When they have walked away from their car, they flick their alarm on, making that loud horn sound. They don't have it blow up in their ears, but they don't care what it is doing to the hearing of others. Even when they're moving things around, like their bathroom items, they plop them on the counter, smash them here or there, making all kinds of noise. You know the type.

Certainly, from a psychological perspective, we can all understand that people who behave in this manner are seeking attention. The problem is, while they are seeking attention for that undefined something that is lacking within themselves, they are invading the lives of others. And, this is simply not a good thing. It harms the life of others.

How about you? Do you behave in this manner? Do you know someone who does?

If you do behave in this manner, do you ever consider what your actions are doing to the life of others? Do you care? If you know someone who behaves in this manner, what have their actions done to your life?

At the root of all life, is how you interact with life. At the heart of your life, is what you spread out from you and onto others and the world around you. How do you interact with life? How much of your life do you feel is a very conscious well-defined process verse how much of what you say and do is based in a randomness of unconscious activity?

The truth of living a good life is, affect/effect as few people, and this entire Life Space, in a negative manner as possible.

Truly think about this. What are your actions defined by? What sounds do you project out to the world around you? How do those sounds affect others? Once you know this, what are you going to do about this?

The secret to living a pure and good life is, be as quiet as possible.

IF YOU THINK YOUR PHONE ISN'T LISTENING...

01/Apr/2026 07:31 AM

Kind funny… I just wrote a piece about the fact that YouTube was dumping all this bad, *"Old People Dancein' Goth,"* my direction in the late night… Then, post the blog, plus I even had a talk with someone about that something, the next night comes around. And…

I have always known my phone is listening. I mean, there has long been a lot of talk and a lot of internet gossip about the subject. But really, haven't you ever noticed that you're talking about a subject of something—discussing something with someone and then the next day, or sooner, that something pops up in your feed?

Anyway… Post a bottle of the grape (or two) gone down, I hit over to the late-night feed on one of my YouTube Channels. What is presented to me? A grouping of some really great, very obscure, Goth/Dark Wave music. No old and dancing involved. Sure, I was hit with one commercial after the other. Internet hear me! Pease, turn off all of those YouTube commercials!!! But, the music was great. Great, from bands I never even knew about. So yes, they are still out there.

What does this all mean in the reality of our reality? I think we already know. Our phones are listening. Sometimes, they provide us with exactly what we are seeking. But, does that grand reality of our phones listening to our speech truly understand our needs? I don't know???

Think about this for a moment. Think about if someone heard something you said. Would they know the true you? Would, *"It,"* actually understand what you desired? Maybe, yes. Maybe, no.

I believe this all comes down to the fact of words. Think about it. How much do you really ponder about the words that you say before you say them? Do you truly calculate what impact how what you say will influence your reality, that other person's reality, and the general reality that surrounds all of us? I am sure most people never question any of this. Do you?

But, if you do, what do you think about what you say? What do you deliberate about how what you say will impact your next Life-Movement or impact the life and/or the everything of anyone else who listens to what you speak about?

Here's the reality… Your phone hears you. Though all of the whatever's out there may claim this is not the case. It is all so self-proven. As it is self-proven, what are you going to do about it/what are you going to do with it? How will what you say affect the next step in your realty? How will what you say affect the next step in the reality of that individual you are speaking about? How will what you say affect the grander reality of this Life Everything.

It's not so much, you are what you eat. It's more, you are what you say because that is what constructs your reality.

A LOT OF OLD GOTHS
31/Mar/2026 08:21 AM

Kind of funny, I guess… In that, *"I guess,"* sort of way…

My lady, this late PM, questioned me about the music I was listening to on the screen of the TV in the after-hours nonsense that is my night. But, like I told her, *"Amazon Prime gets my Goth algorithm way better than does YouTube."* Plus, they also don't have all of those stupid, non-stop commercials. Yet, if you want visuals, late night, YouTube is pretty much all you gots...

You know, I don't really know how to explain this in a politically correct sort of way but, there are way too many aging Goths making music and creating videos. …People that are way too old to be steppin' in front of the camera, dancing around like they're twenty, and all of that kind of stuff.

Let me step back just a bit…

As I was folding laundry today. And yes, I do wash and fold my own laundry. Scary, right? Anyway, I pulled up my Amazon Prime algorithm and listened to the music that they claims is, *"My Soundtrack."* It was all right on: The Sisters of Mercy, The Mission, HIM, VV, The 69 Eyes, Twin Tribes, Clan of Xymox, to name only a few of the more known examples…

When I fold-up the laundry, and put the clean clothing in their appropriate drawers, I always kick on the sounds. Prime, just gets it. I can kick back, do my business, and listen to the tunes.

YouTube, on the other hand, they plaster all of these old faces in my face. I just have to flip through them. Move onto something else.

I don't know what it is, really??? Well, I guess I do get it on that certain level of the whatever; people want to be stars. They want their face in the crowd. But, when your face is too old to be broadcast to the crowd, then what? Do you/should you keep hammering it out there? No one wants to look at an old person trying to be young.

You know, a million years ago, I wrote a couple of articles… One was, *"The Scream Queens Are Getting Old."* The other one was, *"No One Wants to See Old People Dance."*

It was sad, really… I thought/realized how these once young beautiful women had sur come to the hands of age. And, don't get me wrong here. I'm not throwing shade. We all get old. Me, I'm sixty-seven. Ask any twenty-year-old about that age and they will tell you that's fucking ancient. But, these women who based their careers on beauty and had now/then become the age of a grandmother, yet they were still out there and trying to be young. I don't know?

The other one/the other article, was based on this aging local TV newscaster I saw entering this nightclub one night, filled to the brim with the young. This was way back in the day. He was old. His wife was old. Yet, they went in there, hit the dance floor, and danced the dance from some age gone past. Danced, trying to be young. But, they were not. No one wants to see old people dance.

Maybe they had fun, I don't know? But, what it presented to the world was… Well… You know…

But, back to the storyline… I mean, the music that came to be defined as Goth, growing out of what was originally titled, *"Death Rock,"* the people from way back then are all around my age or older. The next gen came and they aren't much younger. Sure, I've notice, in the past couple of years there has been this major resurgence of Goth Culture, and that's fine; equally the new and the young. But, what I'm speaking about, and maybe I better get to the point, Act Your Age!

I know some people consider bands like Depeche Mode to be on the fringes of Goth. I never really thought of them like that but… The point being, like three years ago they released a really good song with a music video, Ghosts Again. There, they're doing their business but embracing their age. And, that's a good thing, right? Be who and what you are.

I mean, I believe we all see it every now and then, the old dressing very young; attempting to re-embrace a different time in their life. Or, like the Old Guy who tries to pick up on the young waitress or just the young someone in the Out There. They just make themselves look stupid! Just because a Server smiles at you does not mean they want to hook up. They just want a good tip.

Now, I get the other side of the issue. Me, I feel very young. I certainly do not feel anywhere near the definition of my biological age. But, I don't let that make me pretend I am anything but what I am.

I don't know??? Music Video or not, it's just hard to watch people not realizing their age. What do you think?

INSPIRATION FROM STRANGE SOURCES

30/Mar/2026 09:38 AM

I have long understood that inspiration comes from strange sources. I mean, it comes at you, it inspires, it causes that need to rise up in you to do/to create that something. And, if you do, you do. But, if you don't, you don't.

I believe this is why so many live a life unfulfilled. Inspiration comes at them, but they do nothing about it. They do nothing with it. They do not follow it up or follow it through.

I don't know about you, but on eBay, I have a bunch of alerts set waiting for that something I am looking for to become available. Mostly, these alerts are for very specific books, particular guitars, and/or select watches. But, I have alerts set up for a few other things, as well. One of them, is for my Zen Filmmaking Brother, Donald G. Jackson. Interestingly, there's not a lot of things that pop up defined by his name. But, I guess that's just what being an Abstract Artist is defined by. *"I'm an artist, god damn it,"* as Don used to love to say.

Anyway, and in any case, the other day this book that was written about him, (not by me), popped up. It had been offered on Amazon for a while, a while ago. And, I picked up a copy. First via Kindle, then a softcover. I'm not going to discuss the what's what about that book right here, right now, as you will understand if you keep reading a bit further. But, what I will say is that book was the inspiration that caused me to actually sit down, (during the pandemic lock-down), and create the book I did about, *Donald G. Jackson: Soldier of Cinema.*

When I first read the author's book, which you can now find most of via on-line articles, it caused me to realize that it is true, as he stated, no one had yet detailed the true life of the filmmaker, Donald G. Jackson. But, as the author did not personally know the man, how could he write a true and revealing study of the man. Thus, my motivation was kicked into gear. As whom better to write a book about the life, the philosophy, the ideology, and techniques of Donald G. Jackson than me? Though I will say, Fred Olen Ray, in his book, *Hell-Bent for Hollywood: A Director's Journey* does reveal some very interesting things about Don. Great book!

What I'm saying here… And, I'm just using in the creation of that book, (not Fred's), as an example, inspiration can come at you from strange sources. But, it is you that must choose to do something with that inspiration. Because if you don't, you don't. Then what?

In closing, at least for this bit of this piece, that guy's book initially caused me to write a blog/article that was up on this site for a while, before I actually decide to compose the book about Don. Perhaps you had a chance to read it, perhaps you did not. Either way, here is it is again, for you reading pleasure.

And remember, when inspiration strikes, don't let it pass you by!

The Unauthorized Biography of Donald G. Jackson

By Scott Shaw

Life forever amuses me. The actions of other people also amuse me. Though, in truth, I forever find myself questioning why some people do some of the things that they do…

More often than not, I find that when people contact me to tell me of some of the goings-on out there in the world, I wish that they had not done so. Really people, I just don't want to know! I live this very simple (semi reclusive) life. I focus on art, spirituality, meditation, and helping others whenever I can. All the nonsense that goes on out in the world, I just find distracting.

Anyway, before I get too far off target, let me get to the point. Somebody told me that someone had written a biography about Donald G. Jackson and published it on Amazon. The title, *"From Roller Blade to Frogtown: The Strange Film Journey of Donald G. Jackson."* Interesting title.

So, I popped over to Amazon to check it out. The cover, a photo of Don that I had taken and the author had altered and used without my permission. Does no one care about copyright laws? There's also a frog from Frogtown on the cover, a little silhouette shot of me near the bottom from *Max Hell Frog Warrior,* and a screen grab of one of the nuns from *Roller Blade Warriors.* The Kindle version of the book was only ninety-nine cents so what could I do? I had to read it.

To be fair, the author, Matthew Skelly, clearly states in the introduction to the book, *"Mind you, I didn't write this book to reveal some hidden bombshell that will set the world on fire. There is nothing new or secret here. Everything written here was already out in the open where anyone with a web browser or a library card could unearth it. My goal here is to simply consolidate all of the information about Jackson's life and work, so I can lay it out in a clear timeline."*

Basically, what he did was to scour this website, (scottshaw.com), throw in a brief passage or two from a couple of other sources, get some information from my Zen Film Documentaries, mix all that up in a blender, talk about Don's and my films and that's the book. I imagine it took some time to do all that and I give the guy an A for effort. For the most part, though he does throw a couple of shots, he speaks kindly about Don and myself, and I thank him for that. I also thank him for taking the time and caring enough about the filmmaking of Donald G. Jackson to put the book together. Though, as is always the case with people who write about someone or something when they were not at the sourcepoint of the knowledge, he does get somethings wrong, takes some of what I have written out of context, leaves out some essential facts, states a couple of things that simply are not true, and the timeline he describes or the motivation for some events he writes about is incorrect. This is why I always say, *"I am alive! I was there! I knew the man! I made the movies! If you have any questions, ask me!!!"* And, as I also always say, *"If you want to know the truth, go to the source."* In this case, I am the source.

Skelly did provide footnotes in the book, and they point to my writings and my films, so that's all good. But, this book was obviously written by someone who knows very little about copyright law and the fact that you need to gain formalized permission from an author or a publishing company when you are going to extensively quote or paraphrase a large amount of another author's writings. You need to do this before you publish a book and offer it for sale. The simple explanation of copyright law is, you can't take somebody else's creation and make money off of it. Basically, what this guy has done is to base his writing about Don upon the quotations and the analysis of my writings, and then detail his interpretation of what I have written and add his own description and critique about Don's life and the movies that Don was involved with. But, he was not there! He does not know what actually took place! So, in some cases, his presentation really misses the point of what actually occurred.

Having lived what this author is writing about places me in a weird position. Knowing who Don was, what he was or was not thinking, what he did or did not do at a specific point in time, and what I was or was not thinking or what I did or did not do at a specific point in time leaves me a bit befuddled when reading this book. I mean, I appreciate the fact that this guy took the time to put his book together but as is the case with all unauthorized biographies, the essence of the person that is being written about, and their creative life motivations, is missing from the pages. If a person did not personally know an individual and they did not speak to those of us who did, at best all a work like this becomes is a book report or a term paper. This is not meant as an insult or a harsh critique of the book in any manner. In fact, if I wasn't me, I may have learned something from the book. But, to know the truth about a person, to understand a person, to know the facts about what an individual actually did and why they did what they did you either need to have actually known that person or at least to have spoken to those of us who did. This author did not do that. And, knowing Don the way I did I do know that he would have been very upset about the inaccuracies presented in this book.

I believe that there has always been the faithful who have appreciated and studied the filmmaking of Donald G. Jackson. And, I am glad to see that some new people may find out about his work through this book. Though it is important to state that some of the facts presented in this book are misleading or false. Just keep that in mind if you read it. But, Skelly did care enough about the filmmaking of Donald G. Jackson to take the time to put the book together, so you've got to give him credit for that!

Awh, Hell… After reading the Kindle version of the book and writing this little tidbit, I'm going to buy a paperback copy of the book and put it in the *Zen Filmmaking Archives*… Or, hand it off to my attorney: one or the other. ☺

*   *   *

29/Mar/2026 07:38 AM

If you're not saying something positive what you're saying should not be said.

I WANT MY DONATION BACK!

27/Mar/2026 12:02 PM

Kinda interesting… I was in a thrift store a week or two ago and this elderly gentleman was up at the front desk. He was old and actually sitting in one of those chair/walker things. I could not help but to overhear his conversation. He had donated some stuff the day before and he wanted some of it back. The cashier was nice enough and went and asked about it in the back of the store, but, as she told the man, it had already been shipped out.

I don't know what ever became of the situation. Obviously, the guy couldn't get his stuff back. So???

But, you gotta kinda feel for the old guy. Something got accidentally or intentionally donated, then he realized that it could never be replaced, and he hoped to get it back. But, when it's gone, it's gone. And, when something is gone, it can never be replaced.

I remember a number of years ago, I witnessed a similar situation. This was back when I was avidly seeking out and collecting rare vinyl.

I was looking through the LPs at this one shop, and this guy came in all up in arms. He had apparently donated some records the day before, and in them was his Kris Kristofferson collection. He wanted them back. But, for whatever reason, the shop didn't have them anymore and, due to their policies, they couldn't/wouldn't give them back to him if they did. He was pissed. Before he raged out the door, he asked me, *"Any Kristofferson in there?" "Nope."*

Today, I dropped off a load of clothing and other donation items at one of my semi-local shops. I like to keep things moving along when I am not going to use whatever-it-is anymore. In there, along with a lot of other stuff, I donate this puffer jacket. It was really nice. I totally remember when I originally bought it. But, the only time I had ever worn it was this one winter when I was in Paris. It never gets cold enough for it here in L.A. So, it was just hanging there in my closet, taking up space. I thought I'd move it along.

The funny thought that came to mind, after I donated it was, *"Just think, someone is going to get a jacket owned by Scott Shaw and worn in Paris."*

Now, I get it, most people could care less about that fact. They just got a really nice jacket for cheap. In my mind, however, that jacket was a Some Thing. It held a point in my memory that will always be there. But, the next person who gets it will never know its origin.

As an avid Thrifter for forever, though I actually rarely buy stuff, but when I do, there have been a few times when I have purchased something that was once owned by a celebrity. It would take way too long to explain why or how I knew that, but I did. Did I care? No, not really. But, it was just kind of an interesting curiosity. You know what I mean…

I guess the point in all of this is, think about the things you own and who will own them after you. Think about the things you own that were one time owned by someone else.

For example, I know when I buy a, *"Used,"* guitar. And, I really don't like that term. But… The moment I begin playing it, in every single case that has ever been the case, my playing style changes, if only for a few moments. It's like the player who owned it before me is communicate to me through the guitar and I play in their style. Or, the guitar has been indoctrinated into a something baked into the realms of ethereal reality and that is all that it knows, so that is how it causes me to play.

So again, think about the things you give away and who will get them after you. What will be the energy karma in all of that? Think about the things you get, and maybe even more importantly, who possessed them before you did. What will they cause you to feel and to do?

Everything possesses an energy. What energy are you giving out and what energy are you taking in?

PAINTING RESTORATION

26/Mar/2026 07:32 AM

I bumped into one of my thrift store buddies today at this one shop I like to go to. At one point, she noticed a painting sitting high up on a shelf and asked me if I could grab it down for her. Happily, I did so.

In checking it out, she noticed a few flaws/scratches in the paint.

That's the problem with thrift store art. Sometimes the people donating it or the staff just don't take care of the art piece, respecting the art, and doing their job with some level of perfection. Thus, paintings get damaged.

I checked it out, studied the canvas, and stuff. It was a nice piece. An old-school landscape, painted by an artist operating from a mature perspective. From examining the canvas, it looked to be from the late 1940s or early 1950s. Unsigned.

In terms of the scraping, I told her that sometimes when I have purchased thrift store art, I have had to touch the art up. It's no biggy. In fact, I like to do it. Break out the oils and match the colors just perfectly. I guess I should have been an art restorer. But, too late now. ☺

We both noticed that the stretcher bars and the front of the canvas had, what looked to be, drilled holes in three points. Don't know what that was all about? Maybe someone just screwed it into the wall? Sad, really. Killing a piece of art like that.

So, here's the question, how caringly do you take care of your art? How well do you take care of the art of others? Do you even care about it? Do you care that the piece of art was inspired, envisioned, and then created with all of the process it took to bring that piece of art into reality? Or, do you just like or dislike it? Maybe toss it in a bin to be donated? Let it get scraped up. Or, worse yet, drilled, and screw into the wall.

I think it's sad the way some people treat art. There it was this painting that was very well done, painted decades ago. Now, just being uncared for.

My thrift store buddy, she decided not to go for it, with the what looked to be drilled holes. I get it. Scrapes in the paint I can touch up. Touch up so no one would ever know they happened. I would have been happy to have done that for her. Holes drilled in and through the canvas, however, that's a different story. That's a hard fix.

This is all just something for you to think about. How do you treat art? Really, how do you treat art? No matter what type or style that art is? If all you do is judge it, maybe use it, then toss it away, caring not what happens to it, what does that do to the heart of the artist, the creators that they have made? And, even more importantly, what does that do to the entire landscape of art? The place where much of the beauty of this life is humanly created?

If you're an artist, you probably immediately get what I'm talking about. If you're not?

Art is art, no matter what form it takes. All works of art should be treated with respect.

Think about it.

*   *   *

25/Mar/2026 01:28 PM

A promise is not a guarantee.

*   *   *

25/Mar/2026 01:27 PM

If you have to ask people for money, via whatever method you do it, there is something wrong with the way you are living your life.

CAST INTO YESTERDAY

25/Mar/2026 06:57 AM

I'm sitting here in the late night. Another bottle of the grape poured down. As those of you who know me, (or know of me), for those of you who know my tales, sometimes before I lay myself down to sleep, I tend to watch the algorithm of late-night music videos that pour upon my YouTube screen.

I took a little detour tonight, however. Decided to change the pace. There was a lot of Dream Pop playing. I've always wondered what's the difference between Dream Pop and Shoegaze? I'm sure there's a definition. But, what really are such definitions? Answer: Just more bullshit, defined by the reality of somebody who doesn't really know.

Anyway, and in any case, a song popped into my brain… You know, one of those songs that's sitting way back there, waiting to be reheard. We all have them. We all remember them. Usually, when we remember them, however, we never seem to have any way to re-play them and let them parade in our ears.

Tonight, that was not the case, however. I could just type it in. And, it would come up.

The song? *Tear Stained Eyes* by the band, Son Volt. Damn! That's a great song.

There's no music video or anything like that that goes along with that song. The band never made one. And, maybe that's the best thing, just allowing the lyrics, and the music, to drive the visions in your mind. It's a perfect experience.

Somehow/someway, while listening to that song, it drove me to thinking about my youth. Youth, at a time when I was rapidly becoming an adult. Maybe way before many/most of those who surrounded me or of those who had walked before me. I was still young. Young, but having walked a long hard road down my (then) short path of life, at that moment of my reality, maybe I was too old for my time? I don't know?

Again, anyway and in any case, the song sent me to thinking about a point—a point when so much of my life was defined by a certain street, Western Ave.

It was a time. I was maybe eleven, twelve, or thirteen. That's the time I lived there. In the area of L.A. now known as K-Town. But, it was a different era of the world back then. That street it held so much/so many of my experience and my realizations. They all happened along that street at that point in history.

Now, I could go into all of that like some sort of autobiography nonsense. But, I'll leave that to another time, and perhaps another author. As. my days are growing short.

Anyway, this flash came to me… Came to me, as I was listening to that exceptional song. It came to me, that I should start out, Western Ave., maybe at Wilshire Blvd. I should take the walk. Walk from the Wiltern Theatre, where I saw so many seminal movies in my youth. Take that walk, North. Walk past all the businesses that have come, that have gone, that are forgotten by most, but not me. Maybe just step back a few feet deeper South down Western. Back to one of the early Hapkido studio where studied. Or, a bit deeper still. The location for, *The Funky Cuts Barber Shop,* as it was called in the very first film where I given the starring role. A piece for a USC film student's final project. Or, more North to the bookstore where I discovered, *The Tao Te Ching.* That book changed my life. Then, walk a little farther to the next theater of cinema, The Embassy, (now long gone). Where again, I saw so many exceptional pieces of film. Keep walking North, up towards Hollywood, where I eventually re-ended up. Born there, lived there, perhaps I'll die there.? Like the lyrics from that great song by, The Animals, *San Franciscan Nights, "I wasn't born there, perhaps I'll die there, there's no place left to go."* Yes, Hollywood has defined me. Perhaps, the most major part of my life.

So, that song, set me to thinking… I should/could continue my walk, past all of the events of my life up that street. Events, that happened along Western Ave.

There was a bike shop. I bought the bicycle that I loved more than any bicycle I had ever owned. Ever owned and ever have owned. And, just a side note here, I have literally flown to Italy and had bicycles created for me. But, I won't go into that here.

Back to the bike I love the most. This beautiful green Schwinn, Pea Picker Model, as it was called. Loved that five-speed Stingray. How long did I own it? A very short period of time. Stolen.

You know, I think that's what most people who steal things never understand. For them, all they do is gain something. But, for the person they take it from, they have robbed an essential element of their life. To this day, and all the bicycles I have owned since that point in time, as I have been an avid bike rider much of my life… There has never been a bike that touched me more deeply.

Okay, Okay… Before I get too far off track. And/plus, I bought a few other bikes from that dealership. But, continuing in the forward motion up Western Blvd. Then, there was Reginald Denny. This great hobby shop. Here, then gone—forgotten by most. But not by me. I lived it.

Now, there were several other places in between. Let's say, between Wilshire, and Hollywood Blvd. Let me state this one particular business, Pioneer Chicken. For some reason, I know not what, there have been all of these photographs, and/or people, discussing Pioneer Chicken on Western Ave. and Hollywood Blvd coming into my feeds. I've even seen a few photos of Bukowski hanging out there. He lived just down the street and around the corner from me, when my mother and I moved back to Hollywood and we lived over on Hobart between Hollywood and Sunset.

That was a place, Pioneer Chicken, where my bud, Saturday Jim (RIP) and I would hit up after a long hard night of Punk Rock Slam Dancing and drinking post living whatever it was we lived at the Punk clubs. We would grab a bucket of their chicken. Make our way back to his aunt's house, just a block away. She was a GREAT gal. We'd drink a couple more beers, shoot a little bit more Jack Daniels as we ate that hallowed chicken. Then, he would crash on the couch. I would grab the reclining chair. Passed out. Drunk beyond belief. Living a reality that few people could ever imagine. God, that was an exceptional time of life! Everything was possible. Everything was so haveable. Now/today, pretty much all the participants of friend-scene, (other than me), are dead. Sad really. All I can do is remember and question why???

Or, speaking of Saturday Jim… We could go up to the end of Western where he planted his head into the wall at the point where Los Felix turns into Western. Venchinzo and I were waiting at their apartment over on Garfield for him to get home one night. We were planning to go and see *The Surf Punks* at the Roxy. Jim didn't show up and didn't show up. Finally, we get a call from the ER. He had gotten way too fucked up with his truck driving bros and while riding his motorcycle home, he didn't make the turn. BAM! Fucked himself up pretty good.

Kinda funny, really… Western now/today, for a few decades actually… I don't live too far from Western over here on the ocean side end of the street. In fact, just yesterday I went to a thrift store that I like located on Western. Kinda crazy, though it is the longest street in L.A., how that street has defined so much of my life.

So, I don't know, what do you think about this? Do you want to take a walk with me down memory lane? Do you want to take a walk along Western Ave. Walk, from Wilshire to Hollywood Blvd. And/or beyond? Maybe we could take a camera and film what is now, as I reminisce about what was then. Maybe we could make a Zen Documentary. I don't know, what do you think?

Life, reality, what does it really mean? I have my memories. You have yours. Which ones are more important?

Me, I can sit here and reminisce. I can sit here and write about them. But, this now is never that then. So, what does that then actually mean in this now?

Question: Should I/are we going to take a walk along that long path of life? I don't know, what do you think?

If nothing else, take a long hard listen to that great song by, Son Volt. It's one of those songs that once you hear, you will never forget it. It's one of those great songs, that I wish I could have created. A song that your mind will always return to. Return to, until you are no more. Then what?

What happens when all your memories are gone?

Like has been said by someone much more wise than I, *"You die twice. Once, when you leave your body. Second, when the last person who remembers you speaks your name no more."*

ZEN FILMMAKING: UNDER THE INFLUENCE

24/Mar/2026 08:12 AM

Kind of funny, in that weird sort of way… I was going to call this piece, *Zen Filmmaking: The Influence Expands.* But, I realized that it would be way better stated, *Zen Filmmaking: Under the Influence.* … Which, I will explain in just a moment.

You know, when Don Jackson and I developed *Zen Filmmaking,* initially it was just a way for us to place a definition on the crazy, abstract, free-form, art-based style of filmmaking that we both embraced. From there, I guess mostly through my writings, somehow, in some way, the understanding spread out and on and forward and all of that kind of stuff. A lot of people began to at least know about it, if not full-on embrace it. At least to some level.

As has been well documented by historians and journalists… I guess I should state here, authentic journalists, the kind that actually wrote/write for real magazines. (Magazines, remember those?), and books, and places like that... Not the kind of dribble that's poured out onto the internet every second of every day. But, and in any case, it has been well documented that *Zen Filmmaking* has influenced a lot of filmmakers; most notably some well-known, professional filmmakers who create projects in the real bastions of filmmaking, not down here, in the bottom tier of the No Budget Realm.

Okay… Stated and noted… *Zen Filmmaking* spread from the minds of Don and myself, and it moved outward from there. We, he and I, me, and others, there have been some crazy films produced via *Zen Filmmaking.* Hey, it's ART, baby!

For whatever reason, the name has meant something to some people. Yes, some have shunned it, while others have embraced it.

This being said, every now and then the title, *Zen Filmmaking* will pop up in an arena that even surprises me. The latest… An entity that falls under that category. Somebody apparently has released a *Zen Filmmaking* beer. No joke.

Now, I can go into the fact that *Zen Filmmaking* is a Registered Trademark. Meaning, legally, you cannot use the term without obtaining authorization; especially when it involves making money off of it. Did they contact me about using the term? Nope. Nor, did they send me a check for my percentage of any of the money they made while selling said named beer. Hell, they didn't even send me a can of the beer. I would love to taste it! You know, just to check it out.

But, beyond all this and that, I do find all this very-very amusing. Amusing, that someone would actually use *Zen Filmmaking* as the name for their beer. Maybe, *Samurai Vampire Bikers from Hell* or *Max Hell Frog Warrior* will come up next. ☺

I don't really know much about the company that released the beer. From what I can figure out, they're based out of Seattle. And, they apparently release limited edition beers, in association with what looks to be a Micro Brewery/Gastropub, or something like that? And then, it looks like they distribute their beers to various places. *Zen Filmmaking Beer* apparently won the International Beer Day Badge at one bar and some other awards at some other locations. Here's the way one consumer described it, *"Near perfect IPA. Dank pine, lemon and grapefruit peel. Strong but not boozy."* I guess I should be proud. But, I probably would have rather gotten paid. ☺

Overall, from a more philosophic perspective, I believe that's the point/hope of all artists—that your art gets out there, in whatever form that may take, and it spreads from there into the minds, and, at least in this case, to the pallets of everyone.

So, if you know anything about this company, and/or maybe know the people that run it, tell them to pay me the money they owe and to send me a can of the beer. I'd love to place it in the *Zen Filmmaking Archives.* At least the can, as I'd have to drink the beer first. ☺

*   *   *

24/Mar/2026 06:42 AM

Do you continue to make the same mistake?

* * *

23/Mar/2026 12:14 PM

You should never let things that aren’t any of your business become your business.

LIVING CONSCIOUSNESS OTHER THAN YOUR OWN

23/Mar/2026 07:45 AM

Most people live in a space of consciousness that is solely defined by their own specific view of reality. They enter life, they pass through their life, yet the only life they even consider is their own. Of course, they will deny this fact. But, in their denial, their truth is revealed.

Right now, ask yourself, who are you thinking about? If you were to describe your upcoming day, what are you doing and why? Truly, look deeply into yourself when answering these questions. What is your true inner motivation for what you are about to do?

For some, they may state that they are thinking about their family, and what they are doing they are doing for them: be that going to work, cleaning the house, or whatever. But, look deeper, and who is at the inception point of that proclamation? It is <u>they</u> thinking about them. It is <u>they</u> believe that what they are doing they are doing for them. It is <u>they</u> that desired them in the first place.

Mental situations like this also occur when a person is perhaps young and in love. All they think about is that other individual. All they want to do is that other individual. But, at the sourcepoint in all of this is the fact that the person is, *"In love."* That part of them is being simulated by that other individual. Therefore, they are willing to do anything to keep that feeling alive. Thus, who are they really doing what for and why?

Most people never contemplate any of this. They never question the why they do what they do. Do you?

There are some people, (few in numbers), that actually go out of their way and walk a pathway of very consciously trying to help others. But, here is where all of this gets very complicated. Why are they doing it? What is their reasoning? And, what is their reward? The fact being, virtually no one chooses to do anything unless there is some form of payment or reward.

We could look to those who do bad and hurtful things to others in this scenario. But, I believe, we can all agree that anyone who operates from that life-perspective is functioning at the lowest level of human consciousness. So, at least within this piece, we do not need to peer into their mindset.

It is all of the others that pass through their life with very little predetermined thought or ideology that we should study. Who are they thinking about and why? What is motivating their actions and why? In fact, what we really need to study is, what makes you do what you do and why? And, how often do you think or even care about how your action will affect others?

Most people exist throughout their life based upon a very selfish perspective. Though most will deny this fact, it is, none-the-less, a fact.

Truly take a long hard look at yourself—a long hard look at the things you have done in your life, and the things you are planning to do. Who is at your helm and what is the motivation?

So, what are you going to do next and why are you going to do it? Who will it benefit? Who will it hurt? And, why are you doing any of it?

Ask yourself these questions before you ever do anything. Maybe they will not only make you a more conscious individual, but it may even help the overall landscape of the world to become a better place.

*   *   *

23/Mar/2026 07:44 AM

No matter how far you walk down any road looking for something, if what you are seeking doesn’t exist on that pathway you will never find it.

* * *

23/Mar/2026 07:43 AM

The people who doubt or criticize the accomplishments of others possess a mindset based upon their own lack of accomplishment.

STATES OF CONSCIOUSNESS

19/Mar/2026 07:45 AM

Most people pass through their life without giving much thought to what level of human consciousness they are existing within. Some people think they're smart. Some people think they're dumb people. Some people think that someone else is smart. Some people think that someone else is dumb. Some may even think that a specific individual is a very good person or perhaps even a very bad person. But, the thing that few people ever contemplate is what level of consciousness a specific individual is existing within.

Since the dawn of man, there has been those who have followed the higher path of understanding. Most, have followed this path via, *"Religion."* And, I put the term religion within quotation marks for a very specific reason, as it is a very specific thing.

There are many ancient religions that have flourished since the dawn of the human race. It seems people, by their very nature, want and/or need something greater than themselves to believe in. There is the Vedic religion which led to Hinduism, which led to Buddhism. There is Judaism which laid the foundations for Christianity. As time has progressed, other new religions have arisen. To name just a few: Islam, Mormonism, Scientology, and I'm sure there are hundreds of others.

Each of these religions tell their participants they must behave in a certain manner if they wish to reach the highest goal of that particular system of belief. For Hindus and Buddhists, that goal is enlightenment. For Christians, that goal is to go to heaven when they pass from this life. For Islam, it is paradise. I am told, for Mormonism, it is that they will receive their own planet if they have been a true and faithful servant of the religion. Thus, all religions are based in methods that are designed to make the individual a good person, defined by the parameters of that specific system of faith. What is missing however, is the study of the states of consciousness.

First of all, take a look at the various religions, analyzing them from a distance. On the grand scale, where do you believe the aspirants within that specific religious grouping dwell? What level of consciousness do they possess?

Now, here's a harder question. At least gaged by your level of truth. Where do you believe you dwell on the levels of advancing consciousness? Be honest with yourself. Where are you positioned in the advancing realms of human consciousness?

Throughout the centuries, various religions and philosophic groups have defined various means in order to describe what level of consciousness an individual is existing within. Certainly, the theory of Chakras is one of the easiest to understand.

From Sanskrit, the word, *"Chakra,"* literally means, *"Wheel."* This term refers to, *"The wheel of human existence."* Or, more precisely, *"The movement of human consciousness."*

As you may know, there are believed to be seven Chakras in the human body. They rise upwards from the base of the spine to the top of the skull. I've written extensively about the understanding of the Chakras, in places like my book, *Yoga: A Spiritual Guidebook,* and elsewhere. So, I won't rehash all of that here. What I will say is that a system such as the understanding of the Charkas at least provides people with a means to gage their own level of human interaction, awareness, and consciousness.

So, here arises the question. Asked again, what level of consciousness do you exist at? And, how do you gage yourself, (and others), as a means to come to a deeper understanding of, not only your own reality, but the reality that is vibrating around you?

Most people never think about any of this. From my perspective, what occurs due to this fact, is that no one advances. There is no level of personal growth. Why? Because if you do not think about this subject—if you do not take your own personal level of advancing human consciousnesses to heart, then there is no growth.

The question then comes down to, do you actually care about your own physical, psychological, and metaphysical advancement? If you do not, like most people in their life, then do nothing. But, if you do, then you need to find a pathway to cause your consciousness to grow in a positive manner.

So, what are you going to do next?

THE ESSENCE OF MEDITATION

18/Mar/2026 08:48 AM

Have you ever attempted to meditate? I'm not just speaking about the one or two times you have sat down and closed your eyes. I'm asking you, have you ever set up a regiment of meditation and done it on a day-to-day basis? If you have good for you! Most people have not.

The thing about meditation is, I would imagine everyone has heard about t. Maybe some people have actually tired it out. But, few people have ever set about on a course to actually learn how to truly meditate. And, I used the term, *"Learn,"* very descriptively.

As a martial artist, for virtually all of my life, I have noticed how the non-martial artist always assumes that meditation is part and parcel with the practice. The fact is, to this day, I have never met a professional marital artist who actually meditates. Sure, maybe at the end of their classes they tell their student to sit down, cross their legs, and close their eyes. But, this only lasts for a couple of minutes at most. People, that is not meditating!

The other thing about meditation that people commonly assume is that it is some calm state of mind that is easily achieved. At least at the outset, this is not the case, however.

You can sit down and close your eyes. You can consciously try to focus your mind. But, without a specific pattern of finding that inner-place all you are doing is diving deeper into your thoughts.

This is where the Mind Game of meditation arises. Just because you believe you are meditating does not mean that you are meditating.

This is the trick of the mind. Many people believe that they are meditating when they are simply allowing the mind to be dragged deeper into a passive pattern of thought. But thought is not meditation. Thought is only thought.

Meditation is a very tricky subject. And, it sends many so-called meditators down a path that leads to very little.

The thing about meditation is, the process is a long in-depth and involved training procedure that few people possess the mindset for. This is why I often ask people if they meditate when we are developing a relationship. This question does not come from a position of judgement, just a place of curiosity. Because, if a person does meditate, you can quickly understand, at least at a rudimentary level, who and what they are—what their life is about.

And certainly, everyone who focuses their life on a conscious pattern of integrating meditation into their existence is not instantly a person of the highest standing. But, if an individual is willing to put that type of mental focus into their daily practice, you can get a window into their personality.

But, what is meditation? In brief, it is a process of silencing the mind. Why should one do it? There are tons of reasons that have been propagated throughout the centuries. But, the one thing that I will say is, the moment you met the space of No Thought you completely understand why it is such an essential tool to the development, spiritual and otherwise, of your life.

In life, we are all taught to think, to focus, to fantasizes, to whatever… All across the globe, throughout time, thinking has been the key component to living, daydreaming, and achieving. Everybody does it. They do it without a thought. But, for those few that wish to find the Deeper Mind, the technique for that, at least one of them, is via meditation.

Here comes the question, do you care about finding that Deeper Mind? Do you care about understand what all of the sages throughout history have been discussing? Do you wish to come to a new and deeper understanding of yourself?

Do you wish to find mysticism? If you do, then maybe it is time to truly learn how to meditate.

Like all things: your life, your choice.

*   *   *

17/Mar/2026 12:37 PM

If all you look for is the dirt, you will never see what is clean.

HOW DO YOU SEE YOURSELF?

17/Mar/2026 09:23 AM

How do you see yourself? No really, how do you see yourself? When you look in the mirror what do you see?

Now, think about this, how do other people see you? When they look at you, what do they see? How would they describe you?

Is how you see yourself, the same as how other people view you?

In life, each person has a projection of themselves. They see themselves the way they see themselves. For some, when they look in the mirror, what they see is based in positivity. For others, when they look in the mirror, what they see is based in negativity. They like what they see, or they do not like what they see.

For some, life is all about their physical appearance. This is why so much money is spent on plastic surgery and the all kinds of the everything else that goes into that which is on the outside.

But, there is a deeper study in all of this. When you look to your self, when you look to your internal working: what do you find in your mind, how you think, what you think, your desires, your emotions, and all the whatever that causes you behave the way you behave and to do what you do? Look deeply, what do you see?

Isn't that subject even more important of an investigation than simply the external?

But, think how few people even contemplate that subject.

Once upon a time, in human history, not all that long ago, inner-exploration was on the tongues of everyone. Now, it has been case aside. But, the physical, the seen, that is seemingly a never-ending story.

As a filmmaker, ever since I first got into the game, image was so important. I think to when I was casting a film,

I would receive tons-and-tons of headshot. A picture never lies, right? Wrong. There was so many times that the actor or actress would arrive for their audition and they looked nothing like their headshot. I would often jokingly say, *"I want to meet the person that's in this photo."* The question then becomes, is that how they actually saw themselves or was that simply a ploy to get them through the front door?

And, that's the thing… …That's what brings us back to the question at hand, how do you see yourself? Do you see yourself as you truly are, or do you see some altered image visible only to your own mind? Do you do this on the physical level, and do you do it on the internal level? And, how honest are you with what you find—what is actually there?

This is an important subject. You should really think it through.

I DON'T READ MY DMS

16/Mar/2026 03:18 PM

Kind of funny, I suppose… For some strange reason today, I can't really tell you why, I decided to look at my DM's on IG. This is something that I virtually never do. Why? I really don't have an answer. I just don't do it.

Anyway, I noticed that there was this one DM, and I read it over. It was telling me that somebody, (of very important status), wanted to speak with me. I thought, okay, I'll definitely respond to that DM. Let me think about my answer a little bit, because I want to say a few of the right words to the sender, and then I'll hit them up tomorrow. Tomorrow being today.

Today, I get all my thoughts in order, and I'm ready to hit 'em up. I read over the DM again, and I realized, it was written twenty-seven weeks ago. I laughed to myself. All the thought I'd put into the message, and it all meant nothing. You know, twenty-seven weeks, it's just too late to reply. So, I let it go. Sorry to the sender!

In another instance, I noticed that somebody had hit me up telling me that I was an inspiration to them in the world of filmmaking. And, they hoped I would keep making films forever. Very nice thought. Thanks! When did they write that? Two years ago.

It's kind of like when people ask me for my telephone number these day… I just don't do that anymore. As I explain to them, I don't answer my phone. I don't listen to my voicemails. And, I don't respond to texts. I've been like this for a very long time now. Thus, only a few of my very close people have my phone number.

I always detail to the people that ask, it's just the method to keep you from getting mad at me, due to all of the reasons I have just explained.

I remember back in the day, when I used to give out my phone number to people that would ask, and then I would never respond, they'd get all pissed off at me. They'd take it all personal. So, to just keep that melodrama from happening, now, the only people that have it are the people I'm going to actually answer the phone for, listen to the voicemail from, or respond to the text. So, if you have my number, you should feel pretty lucky.

Life in the world of modern communications. I'm mean, the truth be told, I really have to play around to even figure out how to read my DMs on IG as I so rarely even try. My fault.

I've been around a long time. The telephone used to the be the main method of distant communication. If you were home, you would answer. Not home, they would have to try later.

I remember the reason I finally bought an answering machine, you know one of those very old-school analogue one's with tape. It was because I had given one of my guitars to Valdez Guitars on Sunset, way back in the way back when. They were the place to have all of your refinishing and customizing work done back in the day. Anyway, I get a phone call one afternoon, and they were really incensed that they'd been trying to get in touch with me for like two weeks as my guitar had been completed.

It was this really cool Gibson SG that I had back in the day. Back then, I predominately only played SGs. I had brought it in for a refinish, and they were such great craftsman that they actually put a veneer on the top before they did the refin. Plus, they did a great job on the frets and with installing these new DiMarzio Super Distortion pickups that had just hit the market. I wanted them installed with a coil splitter switch and a phase switch. That's the kind of stuff we used to have done back in the day... Anyway, they really did a great job. But, they'd apparently been trying to get in touch with me forever. Thus, they wanted to get paid. I immediately drove up from Manhattan Beach, where I was living at the time, through all of the L.A. afternoon traffic.

Anyway, that's just a memory from the old school and the way communication used to be communicated. Then, came pagers, definitely had one of those. Then came voicemails on the pagers. Had one of those, as well. That was the main Hollywood communication accessory back in the day. Then cell phones hit the world, and everything changed. Particularly, when the smartphone was invented.

Just a walk down memory lane. Sorry!

Oh wait, I skipped the FAX machine. Never mind…

So here we are, in this modern age, there's all kinds of different ways to communicate with one another. Though I post on Instagram, (sometimes), Facebook, TikTok, X (never). I just never have really used them as a means of communication. So, will I start to look at my DM's a little bit more after this experience? I don't know. Maybe? But, probably not. ☺

IN FOR A PENNY, IN FOR A POUND

16/Mar/2026 08:23 AM

Tell me, how much full-on effort have you put into anything in your life? How many things have you gone all-in for, doing what you must do until you reach your end-goal?

For many/most they do very little. They may try a little bit of this or of a little bit of that, but then it ends. The work has been completed without ever having been completed.

For some, their job is another subject all together. They are told what to do, so they do it, knowing that if they do not do it, they may lose their job. Great motivator. But, what does all of that worker bee mentality equal at the end of their days? They came, the saw, they conquered, but it was not for them. Sure, maybe they made some money doing it. Sure, maybe they kept their job. Sure, maybe they made their company that much bigger and better, but what did it do for the essence of their life? Think how many people spend their entire lifetime living in a perpetual sub-misery based upon the job they must do day in and day out.

There are some people that follow a path towards its end. Maybe they go to school and get a degree or a certification or a something and then they leave that school environment intending to put that certificate to good use. But, once in the real world, they decide it's not for them. They leave that path behind. So, what did all of that study truly equal?

Many/most people have no idea what they wish to do with their life. They simply pass from birth to death with no true direction; guided by whatever desires and influences they find themselves surrounded by. How does that affect the ultimate evolution of anything, not to mention the evolution of their (your) own life?

Truly, take a moment right now and take a long hard look at yourself. First, look back to your youth, what did you plan to achieve? Did you achieve it? Then, look at your mid-life, what were you intending to do? Did you do it? Finally, look at your here and your now, what is it that you hope to realize and/or accomplish? What are you truly doing about it?

I often speak about life, what people do, why they do it, and how they do it. I commonly discuss that if everything one pursues is not based in a mindset and a position of goodness and positivity then there will eventually be a price to pay. Every now and then I throw in the concept of karma. But, karma is nothing more than the responsive echo of what each individual does. And, this is where the root of possessing a desire to accomplish anything gets very complicated.

Everything you do, whether consciously or unconsciously, creates that reverberating echo of karma. If what you do is focused, then its slap-back is large. If what you do is minor, then its repercussions are less invasive. But, they are nonetheless there.

Most people when they desire to go after that something never look beyond their Self and contemplate the impact that pursuit will have on other people, mother nature, this planet, this whatever. They just do. And, from this, whether they reach their end goal or not, they have unleashed a wake of creating that reverberating something: be it good, bad, or otherwise.

Truly, think about a time when you were pursuing whatever it was you were going after. Did you consider the impact of that action on the all and the anything else? Did you even care? Or, did you just go after it?

If you achieved it, did it answer all of the dreams you had hoped for? Even more precisely, in looking back, whose life did you impact in either a positive or a negative manner while you were locked into your pursuit?

Most people have a dream of achieving that something. Few people achieve that dream. They simply do not possess the drive or the means to do it. But, in all of this life pursuit stuff, how many people actually consider the all and the everything of anything they are doing and what their doing is doing to others?

How about you? Why don't you take a moment right now and chart all of this out.

You may ask, *"Why should I?"* Answer: Because if you don't take all of this to a personal level and truly understand the impact of all that you are doing and have done—study all that you will do, then you will be doing nothing more than instigating a reverberating karma that never leads you towards living your dream but just adds to the chaos of this place we call, *"Life."*

THROUGH THE EYES OF OTHER PEOPLE

14/Mar/2026 06:16 PM

As those of you have been into this blog for a bit, you will already know, sometimes in the late night, I like to sit back with a glass of the grape and let the algorithm on YouTube run me around the various forms of music videos, in the style of music, I like.

I don't really know why, but one night, a little while back, up pops this young female pop singer, crooning in German. It was good stuff. Very dance/poppy. I mean, I'm usually more interested in watching music videos based in Goth and Dark Wave. But…

Anyway, the algorithm took hold and a few of her videos came through. And, in some of them she and her girlfriends are smoking. PS: She apparently hails from Berlin. A city that I love. But, a city where I cannot place in my mind any other location on the globe where I have witnessed more people smoking. I mean it's everybody, everywhere, all the time.

…I've spoken about that in a blog a little while back.

The singer, she's obviously gay, as all of her interests and castmates are also young attractive woman. All good! Smoking and gay. None of my business. But, by placing her truths in front of my eyes, it has, at least, allowed me to view the world in which she dwells.

You know, I forever find it interesting how people like to attach their definitions, their judgments, their ideas, their dogma, their condescending misunderstandings of another person's reality onto them and evaluate, and maybe even condemn them, from a perspective of their own mind. Do you do that?

But, here's the thing, you can love or you can hate what someone else is doing. You can like it or not. It can make you happy or it can make you sad. But, the one thing you will never understand is the truth that exists in that other individual's being. You will never truly know who they are or why they do what they do. Do you understand that? Or, do you just cast your blanket judgment?

From a personal perspective, (an expression I seem to be using a lot of late), like I have long said, *"They're the ones talking about me, I'm not the one talking about them."* Since the moment I started creating or teaching or whatevering, people have been throwing the condemnations my direction. Yes, some have also loved what I've done. Great! Thank you! It just seems that those who base their life in negativity and being judgmental are the most vocal.

But, here's a question for you, is there any less judgement in loving verses hating?

How about you? Do you do that? How about you? Has that been done to you?

I think we all can learn from this. I believe we all can dive deeper into our own psyche and perhaps discover a deeper truth within ourselves.

What do you like? Why do you like it? What do you dislike? Why do you dislike it? And, can you be pure enough within yourself—can you be a pure enough being to allow all people to simply be whom they are, whom they want to be? Or, do you have to gain your strength by deciding and declaring who is right, what is wrong, and that you are the judge and jury and have the need to cast your judgement onto the what you see outside of yourself?

Next time you are about to express your judgement about any other individual, ask yourself, do you truly known anything about the inner workings of their being or are you just another person who is not mindful enough to allow all people to be who and what they are, thus expressing their own unique truth to the world in the way that they most positively can?

THE VALUE OF NO VALUE

13/Mar/2026 12:48 PM

I don't know about you, but around here, everywhere I look, people are carrying Trader Joe's totes. I mean, even when I go to the airport, people are using the larger versions for carry-on luggage.

The thing is, these totes were, at least initially, made to simply carrying groceries. And, they're really good for that. They're really well made. Many of them are embroidered with the Trader Joe's logo, etc. Plus, they're cheap! I've bought more than a few But, why have they become such a thing?

They even issued some really small ones awhile back. Way too small to do much of anything with. Then, everybody had to have one. They were going for tons of money on eBay and stuff.

My lady she told, the Trader Joe's totes are really sought after in Japan. So, I asked, *"If I bring one of them to my girlfriend in Japan will she really dig it?"* Nervously, she responded, *"Who's your girlfriend in Japan?"* Answer, *"I haven't met her yet, but when I do..."* ☺

I don't know??? If you're living in some other place or something, or you read this at some other point in the future, and you don't know what they are, you can look them online.

I always find phenomenon like this very curious. The value people place on something that really has no value, at least not financially. I mean, again, yeah, they're a great tote bag for groceries. But, look around, they are everywhere. They've become some kind of a symbol of something. What does it all mean?

*   *   *

13/Mar/2026 08:09 AM

We are all defined by what we could have been.

THE UN-ZEN OF MOTORCYCLE ACCIDENTS

12/Mar/2026 12:35 PM

I don't really ride my motorcycle much anymore. Like I've stated probably way too many times, it seems like ever since the pandemic, the moment everybody started to get back on the road, the only person they could think about is themselves. Yep, they're the only one on the road. Everybody else be damned. So, and etcetera, it seems like it's gotten kind of crazy out there. I know, over the last few years, when I have been riding my motorcycle, it's not uncommon that I get run out of a lane, and stuff like that. Having had several motorcycle accidents, one of them life-changing and major, I don't know??? It just makes me question, the question.

Anyway, I hadn't been riding my bike too much lately. So, as it's a warm Winter Day. In fact, I'm told we are at the beginning of a long heat wave. So, even though it's still winter, it is a warm March Day. Being said and such, I decided to go and see if I could start my bike up. Maybe take a ride.

I get over to it. I get it unbundled. Turned it on. No headlight. Not a good sign. I pull out the kick starter, try to kick it over, and nada; nothing. Guess I'm going to have to recharge my battery.

I don't know, maybe it's a good thing? You never know when you're being saved by the Great Beyond. And, that's kind of the thing about all that separate reality stuff. Life versus all that is unknown. Sometimes we're protected. Sometimes, we don't even know it. Thus, we can't really give thanks for it because we don't know it's happening. Nonetheless, sometimes, something is saving us from something. Sadly, I wish that had been the case throughout all of my life—through all of my motorcycle accidents and even beyond. Protected, but not knowing I was being protected.

I guess, for the record, let me detail the motorcycle accidents I've had. As I was sitting here, just a few moments ago, eating my lunch—a nice little bowl of soup. They, the accidents, kind of all flushed through my mind, as I was thinking about my motorcycle, it not starting, and me not riding it.

Anyway, I think my first actual motorcycle accident happened when I was driving on Fountain Avenue, over by LaConte Junior High School. My lady of the time was on the back of the bike, and we had pulled up to this intersection. It was a dirty part of town. It was back then in the 70s, and it still is today. There was a liquor store on the corner. I always remember it. I don't know why? I don't really think I ever went into it. But, I certainly knew it was there.

Anyway, back to the point… I was pulling up to the stop sign and WHAP. The bike just slid right out from under me. My lady and I, BAM. We hit the pavement.

Apparently, what was going on was that somebody had spilled a bunch of oil all over the ground. Where that came from, I have no idea. But, it was slick as fuck. I didn't see it. Thus, I went right through it, and in putting on my brakes, it took the bike out from under me.

Luckily, neither one of us were too badly injured. Did anyone try to stop and help us up off the asphalt? Nope. Not a soul. No one even gave a shit enough to even come over and ask if we were okay. Welcome to Hollywood.

But overall, it was just one of those really annoying situations. And, it hurt! I'm saying we weren't massively injured, but we were both scraped up pretty good. She took it way harder than I.

I think the next time it happened was when I was leaving my martial arts studio. It was in the early afternoon, and I was driving down Reseda Blvd. I had to go and buy something. I forget exactly what it was. But, as I was driving down Reseda, this lady pulled right out in front of me from her parking spot, laying my bike down. Again, though I wasn't without scrapes, it wasn't too horrible of an injury situation.

I remember she was one of those very average middle-aged white women. She gets out of her car. I could tell she really didn't give two fucks about what she had done, or what condition my condition was in. But, nonetheless, she played the part, and we exchanged insurance information, and all of that kind of nonsense.

The next time I went down, I guess it was kind of amusing… At least if you want to see it that way. My friend and I were cruising the Sunset Strip one Saturday night. Back then, In the later 1970s, it was really the place to be. We were both on our bikes, and he saw some pretty young ladies driving in a car with their windows down, and decided to chat them up. He was all playing suave and debonair and all of that kind of stuff. What happened next, well, it wasn't all that much fun. As he was talking, I guess he didn't see where he was going, and he ran his bike straight into mine, sending me flying. And him, he laid his bike out on the street right in front of *Gazzarri's.* The girls he was trying to put his moves on, left laughing their asses off. They just kept on driving, as we had to pick ourselves and our bikes up off the street.

His bike wasn't too badly damaged. Mine, however, had its gas tank completely smashed in. And though it initially started, that was the end of that. It wouldn't really drive any farther. So, I had to coast it down off of the Sunset Strip, onto one of the side streets, and park it until I could go and get my van and pick it up and take it to the shop. Fixing it wasn't cheap.

All in all, those were all pretty minor situations. But, I guess I should have taken note and read the writing on the wall. Next, the motorcycle accident that changed my life forever occurred, a few months later. I was twenty-one years old.

At that point, I was running a martial arts studio, I was attending the university, and as it was a Sunday afternoon, I was going to head over to my mother's to have Sunday night dinner with her. I hopped on my bike, drove maybe a half a mile away, and this young girl of eighteen, driving her parent's Mercedes, didn't see me, and turns left right into me. This sent me flying. Of course, destroyed my bike beyond belief. I still have some photographs of that somewhere in some place. But, more than the bike being destroyed, my skull got fractured in numerous places, and my body basically got fucked hard. And, not in a good way.

I almost died. In fact, they thought I was going to die for the first few days. But then, thanks to the only neurologist in town, as this was a holiday weekend, he lifted the broken skull off of my brain, turned off the bleeding brain, and more or less put me back together. Though obviously, I was never the same.

That was a bad one.

I didn't ride a bike for quite a while after that. But, come the 1980s, and the whole Harley craze, and having spent my entire childhood growing up around Harley Davidsons, it seemed like it was my time to ride again. I bought, and as we all did back then, fully customized a Harley. Spending way too much money!

We had just finished up with *The Roller Blade Seven* and I had just gone up on *Samurai Vampire Bikers from Hell.* I was on my way over to pick up this sweet young lady from her job at a Hollywood camera shop to go and see *Soundgarden.* Never made it. I was driving down La Brea, and a guy didn't see that the light had turned red and he hit me from behind. I went flying onto the payment. The helmet law had gone into effect by that point here in Cali, so at least my head was more or less protected. I doubt it could take another impact.

The ambulance comes. Off to the emergency room I go. All of which I've discussed in other places and at other times, so I won't really go too much into that right now.

I lived. My Harley was destroyed. The guy had no Insurance. His sister was a lawyer. So, once again, I got fucked.

So, off the top of my head, that's the all and the everything of the Scott Shaw motorcycle accidents, at least the big ones.

I don't know… Have you ever been in a serious accident? If you have, maybe you understand. Unfortunately, I've been in a few; both on my motorcycles and in a few cars. None of it is fun. It's always the other guy's fault. And, of course, they don't give a fuck. All they care about is themselves. Yet, if you know the feeling, you understand that you are the one left trying to pick up the pieces of all that is broken.

I guess that's one of the saddest things in life. How so few people actually care about anyone else, and what they're doing to anybody else, once it's been done. All they try to do is to protect their own ass and move as far away as they possibly can away from taking any responsibility for the damage they have created.

How about you? Ever been in a serious motorcycle or auto accident?

How about you? Has something like that ever been your fault? And, if it was, what did you do to fix all that may have been broken?

Life is crazy. We just do what we do. In some cases, what we enjoy doing may very well kill us. All this being said, it doesn't make any of the pain any easier.

Think about it. Think about what you're doing. Think about how you're doing it. Think about what you've done. Think about what you're doing to others. Think about that before you ever think about yourself. Think, are you one of those people that make things better or are you one of those people who hurts and then runs from your responsibility in the situation?

Like I always, all life begins with you. What will you do next?

I don't know if any of this is all that philosophical and/or I doubt that you can grab any deep meaning from it. But, all of this tells us is that we are the sourcepoint for all that we live. We do what we're guided to do and what we desire to do. Sometimes in the all and the everything of that, we may be protected. Protected, when we do not even know we are being protected. But, then there are the other times. The, *"Then What"* times? When all we are left with is to pick up the pieces ourselves—pieces broken by someone else.

WHAT IS TIME?
12/Mar/2026 07:26 AM

I don't know if you have ever noticed this, but I never wear a watch when I'm playing a character in any of my Zen Films. For all of you people out there who claim to be soothsayers and pundits of the truth about the Zen Films of Scott Shaw and/or *Zen Filmmaking,* the one thing that I have never seen mentioned in all of your online, (and previously, in times gone past), magazine raps, is the fact that I never wear a watch in any of my films. This, when I have forever been a lover of fine timepieces.

For many decades now, (commonly), I wear a Rolex or another high-quality Swiss made watch on a day-to-day basis. Did you know that about me? If you did not, then you do not know me! So, stop talking about me! But, in my films, you will never see me wearing a watch, (except in one case when it was part of the costuming). I always take it off before a scene is shot and I put it in my pocket.

Do you ever watch a movie, or perhaps a music video, and you see the person playing a part wearing a watch? I find that very distracting; especially if you can actually see what time it is on the dial of the watch. Then, (perhaps), maybe in another take of the scene, maybe on the reverse shot, there is another time on that watch. Time has ticked on. Distracting! I always look for such things. Do you?

I find all of this very problematic in the creation of, and the watching of a film or a music video. Yes, yes, I know sometimes a specific watch is put on the wrist of character for Product Placement. And yes, sometimes the time is shown in a film for particular story development reasons. But, other than that, I think it's just lazy. It just looks bad. It is distracting.

I mean, I have viewed scenes that are so exquisitely photographed, but then there is that watch on the wrist of one of the character distracting from the wholeness of the all and the cinematic everything.

Come on, what is the purpose of time in a film, a music video, and/or a cinematic whatever? Isn't filmmaking all about the suspension of belief, not what time it is?

This is just all something for you to think about as you travel down the road of life, (especially for you filmmakers out there). This, as you view whatever cinematic creation you may view. What does time have to do with that cinematic whatever, if it does not lead to the development of the story? Why is anyone wearing a watch? True artistic filmmaking is all about the subtleties.

In the world of cinematic art, what is time?

THE GAME OF BLAME

11/Mar/2026 08:10 AM

It's not really an intended process, but it seems like I discus the realities of driving fairly frequently. I guess that's just because, like here in a place like L.A., driving is such an everyday reality. And, while dancing through that reality, a lot of the true human condition is revealed.

For example, the other day, I had pulled up to a four-way intersection where each side had its own stop sign. Okay… You know how it goes, the person who arrived first goes, then the next, and the next.

It was my turn, so I started to drive through the intersection. But instead, this black Mercedes powers through, honking his horn, flipping me off, and I could see he was yelling at me. My turn, not his. But…

I returned the flip off. He drove through. I drove through. And, we were on a way.

The thing is, all this moment of memory did not need to happen. He could have just followed the rules. But, he did not. Me, I did nothing wrong. Yet, he somehow blamed me.

I think this goes to a lot of levels of life. There is all this human activity out there going on. We are all these little ants running around doing what we are doing—believing that what we're doing is oh so important. But, let's face facts. The only person it is important to is ourselves.

Of course, that little intersection thing is a very small blip on the grand scheme of life. But, it does illustrate how people want to shift the blame from themselves onto someone else.

I imagine that we have all encountered situations in life where we have done nothing wrong, yet someone wanted to blame us for what they either created or choose to be a part of.

If you feel like it, maybe take a minute and pull one of those moments up from your memory tape. Take a look at how it was created, what part you took in its creation, and what you did after you were blamed.

...Maybe even remember a time when you blamed someone for something that wasn't their fault. Be honest!

You see, the thing in life is... ...What it all comes down to is... Most people operate from a platform of selfishness. All they think about is only done to make themselves feel and live from a perspective of the things that they wish to feel and live. Thus, even if you are a part of what they are living, before they come to blame you, they wanted that something. Whatever that something may have been. Thus, they were walking, (or driving), on a path to get it. You simply became part of their equation. Then, when it did not go the way they had hoped, they decided to blame someone else; maybe you.

The main thing to do/the main thing to keep in mind, if one of these situations finds you, is that you never want to allow yourself to be sucked into that others individual's melodrama of blame. They want to blame you; sure. Then, let them blame you. Because when it comes down to the fact of the fact, if you did nothing wrong, you did nothing wrong. Don't let them make you do something wrong by allowing them to drag you into their game of blame.

DATA BREACH AKA FAKE FRIENDS

10/Mar/2026 09:38 AM

Have you ever received one of those form letters in the mail where you are told that there was a data breach and that your personal information may have been compromised? I know I have. I've received several of them over the years. Does it worry me? No, not really. I mean, all of our stuff is already out there. Unless you are living totally off the grid, everything about everyone can be found out.

It's like, you give these massive entities your info. They claim they will protect it. They claim all kinds of things. But, the fact of the fact is, you are nothing to them. Just a cog in the wheel, if even that. Do they care about you? No. All they care about is whatever it is they care about. As long as you do nothing to cast a wrong their direction, they never even take you into consideration.

Have you ever had a family member or a close friend do something really fucked up? Maybe even something that negatively affected the evolution of your life. What did you do when that occurred? Did you stand by them? Did you forgive them? Did you help them through it?

…Yes, it may have pissed you off. …Yes, it may have even made you mad at them. But, when all was said and done, did you stand by them?

Did you ever do something wrong to someone else? Maybe it was intentionally, maybe it was unintentionally. But, did you ever do that thing defined by the realms of wrong? If and when you did, who stood by you? Who forgave you? Who helped you reclaim the right in your life and make it past your wrong?

Here lies the definition of a true friend. An individual who actually cares about you. Here lies the definition of who you actually are as a person and whom you care about. Did they stand by you? Did you stand by them?

If we turn this around just a little bit, how many times has some lashed out at you when what you said, what you did, they considered to be wrong? How many times did they refuse to stand by your side? How many times did they try to hurt you back?

How many times has someone done something to you that you consider to be wrong? What was your reaction? Did you immediately shun them? Or, did you forgive them and provide them with a second chance?

I believe for each of us, we have encountered the wrong done by others and the wrong others feel we have done to them. But, it is the what comes next that defines the everything else in the relationship.

Taken a moment. Really think this through. Who has wronged you? What was your next action?

Who have you wronged? What was their next action?

The fact of life is, though many people claim to be your friend, there are actually very few true friends. There are very few people who will forgive you.

Ask yourself, how many people have you forgiven verse how many people you have not?

I get it… People do a lot of fucked up things, all based in a sense of self-worth, selfishness, entitlement, unconsciousness, and all that kind of low mind nonsense. But, as in all life situations: the good, the bad, and the ugly, if you cannot be of the higher mind—if you cannot step beyond the way you demand that another person's life be lived, then what do any of us have? The answer: No One. Just a form letter, coming in the mail, telling us about some very bad thing that they did and, *"Oh whops, sorry."* PS: *"I don't really care about you."*

Think about it…

* * *

10/Mar/2026 09:09 AM

Do you live in a space with your windows wide open, letting the sun shine in?

Or, you live in a space with your curtains closed?

Why?

HATE: THE OLDEST TRICK IN THE BOOK

09/Mar/2026 09:56 AM

I got a chance to rewatch the movie, *"Nuremberg,"* last night. Really good movie. I was very surprised when it didn't win more awards during last year's award season. I mean, the performances are all very strong. The sets and the settings are all very well developed and orchestrated. There is also some very interesting and subtle Under-Story in the film. Plus, the movie really shines light on a very dark point in human history. It really shows how the actions of one man, focusing on the hate and dissatisfaction of an entire nation, can grow an entire movement and cause it to unleash unthinkable tragedy.

And, this is the thing, the movie illustrates how a person who bases their life on dissatisfaction and/or a mindset based upon negativity seemingly easily shifted the mindset of an entire nation in the direction of hate and hurt. Then, taking that negativity and moving it towards unthinkable horrors. Yes, for most of these situations, it's very small things; maybe somebody talking trash behind another person's back and causing others to dislike that person. And that's wrong too! But, all of this mindset can be taken to an entirely different level, like in the case of what took place prior to and during World War II, and make an entire race become the focus of incredible destruction. It's just wrong!

The thing about this mindset is, whether it's on the scale of the German Nationalist Movement, and what was unleashed by its crusade, onto a much smaller scale, where any formalized group of people, whether small or large, if it is based in hate, only negative things will arise.

On a personal level, this is why I always say that you really need to keep your mind only focused on the positive, the helpful, the good, and never on the bad, the judgement, the hurtful, or the negative. The problem with this statement is, however, so many people embrace a state of hate and or negativity and they believe that the actions they take, based upon this mindset, are actually good. They believe that by unleashing this hatred in the direction of one person, one group, one race, one whatever, they are actually doing something good. Look at the Nazi movement. Look at what Pol Pot unleashed. But, the fact the fact is, they are not. It's really simple to see. All you have to do is look at the end result. If someone or something is hurt by any action that is taken, then what is it? What has occurred? The answer is obvious. It is a bad thing. Don't do it!

Right here, right now, this is a good time for you to take a look at yourself. When was the last time you said something negative about a person? When was the last time you said something negative about a situation? When was the last time that those thoughts or actions caused you to do something negative, no matter how right you may have believed those action to be?

Here's the big question, when you did voice that level of negativity, when you did do that potentially hurtful thing, did you even question what you were doing? Did you even have the mental fortitude to actually take a look at what you were creating—while you were speaking that level of negativity/while you were enacting that level of negativity? If you didn't, what does that say about you? And, on the other side of the coin, if you did, you probably would have caught yourself and not instigated any of that negativity at all. Thus, the truth of all reality is in the answer itself. Negativity, badness, hurtfulness, hate, and all that stuff, they all equal the same thing. Nothing good. Period.

All this is just something for you to think about before you speak that next word, before you do that next thing. Ask yourself, is what you are doing based in hate? Is it based in hurtful action? If it is, then you should possess the self-awareness within yourself not to do it.

Hate only equals hate. Hurt only equals hurt. No matter what your motivation, if you are walking down that road, that road will lead to nothing good. You know this. I shouldn't have to say this. Yet, think how many people are still out there trying to hurt.

Hurt equals hurt. Help equals help. Bad equals bad. Good equals good. And mostly, hate is the most dastardly of all reality.

Always spread love. Always speak only the positive. If your reality is based in negativity, If the words coming out of your mouth are based in negativity, judgment, hurtful action, anything like that, possess the mental awareness to stop yourself. Only create the good.

BROWN BANANAS AND SCOTT'S WAFFLE

08/Mar/2026 02:12 PM

My lady and I were having breakfast this morning, and we got onto the subject of bananas. But, I think it's probably best if I get to that matter in just a moment…

Anyway, we were having breakfast... As the story goes, this restaurant always served waffles. But, the way they presented them was very bland. You know, just some butter and syrup and stuff. But, they also offered this very nice presentation of French Toast. The French Toast had all of these great fruits on the top, including bananas. Personally, I'm not a fan of French Toast. …Way too much sugar. But, I had this idea one morning. Why don't I ask them to put all of those fruits and stuff on my waffle. I asked the server if it could be done. She said she would ask the chef. It could and they did. Their waffles became great!

A few times of my asking went by, and their checking if it could be done. The answer was always, *"Yes."* Some time passed and I began to ask for that concoction and the servers no longer had to ask it if could be done, they just knew that it could. A little bit more time went on, and I heard other people asking for their waffles to be made, as it became known, *"French Toast Style."*

I always joking tell my lady, when this occurs, they should have named that waffle, *Scott's Waffle.* You know how some restaurants do; name a dish they serve after a specific person. But nope, they did not do that.

Whenever I hear someone ordering a waffle that style, at this restaurant, I always feel a bit jipped, as I was the one who invented the concept. No credit where credit is due… Kind of the story of my life, I guess. ☺

Okay, that's that part of the story. On to the next…

While we were speaking this AM. …And, talking about bananas. We got to discussing how bananas turn brown so quickly and you never want to eat them like that.

…All mushy and stuff.

With that, a funny memory popped into my brain. A story which I relayed to my lady…

Way back in the way back when, my guru, Swami Satchidananda was coming to town. The mother of the L.A. IYI, (Integral Yoga Institute), Sister Maji, asked me to go and get some bananas for Gurudev at Erewhon, which was, back then, one of the only health food markets in existence. Now, it has become a cultural and tourist hot stop with a few locations. But, this was at its original location.

The thing was, Gurudev only liked to eat very browning bananas. He would not eat the very fresh, yellow kind like most people desire. So, there I was. I go into Erewhon and all the bananas they were offering were very fresh/very yellow. No brown ones. I ask one of the staff members if they had any browning bananas and you can imagine the look in their eyes and what they exclaimed, *"Why would you want old bananas?"* I tried to explain it was for Swami Satchidananda, who was a very well-known spiritual teacher of that era, but no luck all they had/all they would sell me were fresh bananas.

…I did the best I could to pick out the oldest of the bunch.

So, all this becomes/became one of those weird Zen paradoxes in life—a Zen koan. What do you do when all someone/something offers are the freshest of fresh, but all that other person wants is the older and the brown?

Tell me what answer you come up with?

* * *

08/Mar/2026 01:43 PM

If you continue walking the road you are walking, where will you end up?

TRANSCENDING THE OBVIOUS

07/Mar/2026 11:14 PM

What is art? I believe that art for most people means many different things. The one thing that art obviously means is its ability to transcend the realms of the obvious and move towards that deeper understand that is lodged only within in the mind of the artist.

Okay, but what does all of that mean?

I believe that since time immemorial, art has been seen, viewed, listened to, or whatever, and then it was judged. Maybe it was liked, maybe it wasn't. But, at its essence, isn't that the pure representation of art? To be interpreted by the viewer, the listener, the whatever-er?

When the realms of the more abstract began to be embraced within the arts, there came a complete schism, and the basis of the question, what is or is not art? But, here again, at its root, art was and is about two things. One, what the creator envisioned. And two, what the consumer consumed; liking it or not.

But, simply because someone does not like or understand the art of an artist—simple because they do not understand the motivations for the art of the artist, does that take away the art? My answer is, no. Art is created because a person has the vision and the motivation and that whatever else to actually get out there, do what it takes, and get that art created; by whatever medium they may choose. How about you? Do you create art?

For me, my entire life has been based in creating art; via the various methods I have undertaken. Some of the things I have created have been accepted, some have not. And, that's AOK with me. For, at least in my mind, as long as the new creations are being created that is a good thing. That is creativity. That is pushing the envelope of whatever form of art that is embraced forward. I believe this is something that is easily understood by the artist. And, this is why the artist always appreciates the art created by someone else. Maybe they do or do not particularly likc a particular piece of art, but that does not take away the truth of its creation. Again, are you an artist? Do you create art? If you are, then you understand what I am speaking about.

All of this is all just something for you to keep in mind. Constantly ask yourself, is what you are doing creating art? If it is, good for you! If not, that's okay too. Not everyone is an artist. But, in the truth of the truth of art, if someone is doing what they are doing, based in the mindset of art, you should at least be enlightened enough to understand their effort and appreciate that though you may not like what they are creating, what they are doing is, at least, pushing the boundaries of artistic expression forward.

And, isn't that a good thing?

*   *   *

07/Mar/2026 07:09 AM

You can believe you know the truth all you want.

But understand, your truth is not my truth/your truth is not their truth.

Meaning, whatever you believe you believe may be the truth to you but it is a lie to someone else.

THE HOLIEST OF PLACES

06/Mar/2026 01:18 PM

I was popping thought my feed on IG today and this one piece came up about this woman who had traveled to the Great Pyramid of Giza and was totally disappointed. All she did was go on and on about how she had long dreamt of traveling to and exploring the pyramid, but it was inundated with tourist, and she had a horrible time. She spoke about how she made her way to the King's Chamber but the pathway there was totally overrun with tourists. Then she proclaimed, there was nothing powerful or spiritual about the place at all. She warned everyone not to go there. I guess she never read my book, *Zen: Tales from the Journey.*

Well over forty years ago, I traveled to Egypt. At that point in time, the location was not yet overrun with tourism. I, of course, went to the Great Pyramid. This was at a time when you could still climb the pyramids, if that was your desire. Yes, Yes… I understand, that's a bad thing to do. But, at least at that point in time, it seemed like the thing I should do. Which, is something that I did. Sorry!

But more to the point… The pyramids have always been depicted as this great source point of spiritual energy. A place, where one can really commune with the grand beyond, and come into contact with an intense spiritual force. Due to the fact that there were no tourists in the area at the time period when I first went there, I was literally allowed to climb all the way up through the pyramid, and make my way to the King's Chamber, (the center of the pyramid), completely alone. Meaning, I was in the King's Chamber all by myself.

As I stood there, I tried to interact with that promised power-point of energy. Quickly, I realized, however, that it did not exist. If there was any energy within the pyramids, it had been drained a long-long time ago. I talked about this in an essay I wrote for a magazine, way back in the way back when, and later in my book, *Zen: Tales from the Journey.*

Here's the thing… We all hear about the promised spiritual energy in certain locations around the globe. Personally, I've visited many of them. Plus, by the time I ever began traveling to these holy sites, I was already deeply involved in the Spiritual Path. Thus, I knew what I was looking for. But quickly, I realized, from all of these places, whatever may have been there, certainly had been robbed long ago; as was the case with the Great Pyramid.

I've been to where it is said that the Buddha found enlightenment in Bodhgaya, India. I've touched the Ganges River water in nearby Varanasi, (perhaps the holiest city in India), and at its source in Devprayag. I've traveled to monasteries in Tibet. Lived in Rishikesh. I've walked the streets of Old Jerusalem, where Jesus is said to have walked. I've traveled to where the Dead Sea Scrolls were found. Though, I've never been allowed to travel into Mecca… …I guess that's probably because I have blonde hair and I doubt that anyone would believe I'm a Muslim. This, even though my first spiritual initiation was via the Chishti Sect of The Sufi Order. But… I've been to a lot of other places that promise spiritual energy across all faiths all across the globe. Plus, I've been to much lesser-known locations, that are said to possess promised spiritual energy.

The point being, like many people, I've spent my entire life seeking out the spiritual realms and the deeper meanings promised at those locations via spiritual investigation and ultimate emancipation. But, there's nothing there.

A funny sidebar here, if I may… I was actually scheduled to have an audience with the Pope. I was really looking forward to it. But, I received this e-mail. *"The Prefecture of the Papal Household informs you that the following reservation has been cancelled."* Wow! I guess some of his Cardinals or Bishops, or whoever told him what would happen if I arrived in the Vatican. You know, like in all the horror movies, the crosses are going to turn upside down and catch on fire, and the statues of Mother Mary are going to start crying tears of blood and stuff.

I'm just joking, of course. But, I did find that email kind of interesting. I guess it was okay that I could meet with the Dalai Lama, but I'm unworthy to meet the Pope???

The point to all this being, we all expect, anticipate, and are told that there are these spiritually holy places. There are these places of great mystical energy. But, the fact of the fact is, there's nothing there, except for your own projection(s). Some believe. Some don't. Some, like myself, truly seek to investigate and explore the inner hidden realms that are promised at certain places and from certain people.

Speaking of… I've met a lot of people, over my many years walking the Spiritual Path, that we're said to be very spiritual beings. In some cases, I felt it was true. But, in others, I could just see through all the bullshit they were laying out.

The main thing to think about as you pass through life—the main thing to remember is that, just because something is said to be something, that does not make it something. The only something that is something is that something that is revealed solely to you, in your deepest, inner, spiritual being.

Thus, you can go to the pyramids if you want to. They are a great architectural feat. But, if you go there hoping to find some grand spiritual something, some embodiment of power, then, like I said in that essay and that chapter in my book oh so many years ago, the fact be told, if there ever was any great spiritual energy at that location, it was robbed a long, long time ago.

* * *

05/Mar/2026 01:39 PM

Every time you cause someone to hate a person, you have made the world that much worse.

Every time you cause someone to love a person, you have made the world that much better.

* * *

05/Mar/2026 01:38 PM

You can only control what you can control.

*   *   *

05/Mar/2026 06:47 AM

What is your last chance?

*   *   *

04/Mar/2026 02:04 PM

Make a guess… How many days do you have left to live?

What are you going to do with that time you have left?

*   *   *

02/Mar/2026 09:12 AM

How many mistakes have you made?

How much of your life do you consider to have been a mistake?

How many choices have you made that you feel were a mistake?

How many things have you done that you decided later was a mistake?

How many of your life mistakes have you attempted to correct?

How much have you learned from the mistakes you have made?

How much of your life is defined by the mistakes you have made?

A LITTLE BIT CRAZY

27/Feb/2026 09:44 AM

I was watching the news last night and they showed this segment from Japan. There was a little girl having her photo taken by her mother at Shibuya Crossing and some woman, wearing a Covid-style mask, walks up behind the little girl, and with crazed anger in her eyes, she elbows the little girl and knocks her down to the ground and keeps on walking. How fucked up is that?

One of my number one rules in life is, *"Leave the kids alone!"*

Now, for anyone who has been there, or has watch pieces about the location, everybody takes photos at Shibuya Crossing. I even did a Zen Film there kinda recently, *Crossing Shibuya Crossing.* But, for whatever self-distorted reason, this lady didn't like what was taking place and wanted to lash out. Again, who does that to a little kid?

I think back to a time when something similar happened to me. My lady and I were walking down onto the Santa Monica Pier. It was in the later afternoon, on a warm Spring Day. There was a lot of people walking. But, for whatever reason, this guy walking the opposite direction, up and off the pier, decides to focus on me and throw a shoulder into me. You know, shoulder to shoulder. My first thought was, *"Are you kidding me!"* My second thought was, *"I should kick his ass!"* But, that's the thing about knowing that you can kick someone's ass, you don't have to do it.

The thing is, in his eyes, I could see the same thing that I saw in the lady's eyes who went after that little kid. This weird, distorted anger based in some reality that they are living that is alien from the reality of everyone else.

If you think about it, there are a lot of variations to normality. I mean, look around you, maybe even look at yourself, are you normal?

For many, they live in a state of the accepted norm. They live their life, they do what they do, and by studying them, at least from the outside, they are what may be considered, *"Normal."* But, then there are those who exist somewhere off to the side of that definition. Maybe it is based in the small things that they do or maybe it is based in much larger actions. But, however it comes down the pike, they are seen to be, (if I can use a term that may be considered at bit derogatory, but it is very descriptive), *"Crazy."*

Have you ever encountered someone like that? Are you someone like that?

Now, this is where the whole concept of being different or being cursed with mental illness comes into play. There are some forms of this, that have been deemed to demand medication. Those are generally the very exaggerated states. But, then there are those who walk among us, who they seem to function within the realms of (at least) the marginally acceptable. Yet, there is something just not quite right with them.

I mean, some asshole shoulder bumping me is just a joke in my mind. *"What a loser!"* But, had someone knowingly done that to my kid, like what happened in Tokyo, they would have suffered the consequences. And, is the place where all of this kind of stuff jumps off and takes on a whole different meaning. You can be as crazy as you want, as long as your crazy effects no one else. But, the moment what you do does affect someone else, there will be consequences. If not now, sometime in the future.

You know, we all look to medical standards and stuff like that when we encounter people who are a bit off. But, the thing is, the people who do these negative things, do them based upon their own altered psychology. They have a reason for doing what they do. But, if that reason is off-center, then what? What does it do to all of those they affect by the doing what they do? And, this is where all of the excuses of mental illness come into play. I mean, think how many lives have been fucked up and how many people have been sent down a dark road instigated by someone who is not mentally sound.

Years back, in this blog, I would speak about how I had this neighbor who claimed to be some sort of a spiritual something and the conduit for this particular archangel. He was selling his wares wherever he could. But, when he wasn't blasting his bullshit out the windows, he would go into some self-induced rage and, while stomping on the floor, he would scream, *"Fuck me, fuck me, fuck me and mine,"* over and over and over again. The dude was deranged! And, in his actions he messed up the life of all of his neighbors, including me. I had to live next to him for two and a half years before I finally moved. I'm still suffering from the effects of his life derailing actions. Thus, mental illness, *"Crazy,"* is never an excuse. But, it can hurt the life of many people.

Just like if I would have decided to kick the ass of that guy who shoulder bumped me. That probably would have gotten me arrested. Arrested, for something that the other guy instigated.

So, here's the thing, crazy people are all over the place. Many of them are hiding in there seeming normality. I can say, *"Steer clear of them."* But, like the poor little girl getting her photo taken at Shibuya Crossing, they may come at you out of nowhere. And, who knows how that crazed lady's action will affect the overall life of that young girl?

Here we are. We live in this reality. For those of us who care enough to care, we try to do good things, hurt no one, help people whenever we can, and make this life space as good as it can be. Then, there are those who are a little crazy. We can't control them or their actions. All we can do is remain as positive and as pure as is possible and not let them control how we react.

Be good. Hurt no one EVER. That's all I can say. And, if you do meet crazy, try to not let it overtake your life.

Be more than that person who is less.

REACHING FOR THE STARS

26/Feb/2026 09:54 AM

I believe that everybody wants to be successful in life. Very few people actually desire to fail. Do you know of any? Though certainly, the majority of the world's population seems to be very good at the craft of chasing their desires for achievement, what many/most lives end up embracing is the hard truth that what they are living is not all that they had hoped for.

I think a really interesting reality was born a few decades back with the birth of the Internet. I mean, Once Upon a Time it was pretty much clearly dictated that you had to be in one of the major urban centers if you hoped to Make It Big. Bring on the Internet, and instantly anybody could get famous, no matter where they were based.

That's a good thing, right?

Within that, and without that, there also arose an interesting paradigm. Many people, instead of simply working and chasing their fame of and for themselves, instead they decided to attempt to make their claim to fame based on the reality of someone else.

Like I've long said, if you're making a name for yourself by either discussing someone else and/or what they do or create, you are really creating nothing. At best, all you're doing is churning the Word Soup that permeates the reality of all those who have not achieved. Thus, what does any of that—any of what you are doing, really add up to?

As I write this, I think to people such as Peter Fonda. In reading his autobiography, you really take note of the fact that a lot of people were discussing his family and himself in the press and elsewhere. And, in virtually all cases, those people who were doing all of the discussing, were generally wrong in their appraisal. Yet, in their doing, they were allowed to make money by writing an article, a biography, a whatever. When you read an autobiography like his, it really brings home the fact of how little people really know about the truth of anyone else's reality.

I mean, think about it, how much time do you spend focusing on someone else: what they've done, what they've achieved, what they've created, who they've loved, who they've hated, if you love them, or if you hate them... Compare that to how much time do you spend creating your own greatness? I mean really, how does any of that Out Talking affect any element of the truth of your being?

I know in my own life, (and I'm just using myself as an example), I've met people who actually were looking for someone to be mad at. I always thought this was the strangest reality. I would meet somebody. Maybe we would hang out for a while: do some lunches, go to the movies, maybe even make a movie or two, jam some music, whatever... But then, at the end of the day, they would be seeking a reason to become angry, and since I was the closest person at hand, they would decide to focus that anger on me. From that, they did all kinds of dastardly deeds: speaking all kinds of untruths and doing whatever it is they could do to sully my name. But, what were they doing? What were they achieving? Were they making anything any better? Were they making their own reality better? Were they making my reality better? Were they making the reality of anybody who would listen to their prefocused anger any better? No, I don't think so.

It's kind of like you hear about it all the time, people talking... People talk all kinds of trash about somebody that they choose to focus on. An individual that they have or have not met. They think they know what they're talking about, but all they're doing is creating a bunch of negativity. But ultimately, what happens by embracing that level of negativity? The answer is, nothing more than negativity. And, that negativity inevitability comes back on the person who initially instigated it. That's just the reality of reality. Love it or hate it, that is the truth.

So, what am I talking about here? What I'm talking about is that life is a creative process. You can make that creativity your focus. You can dream to become that whatever you wish to become and then pursue becoming that whatever. You can do that from wherever you are now. You don't have to move to the big city anymore. At least, if you don't want to.

I mean, I get asked the same questions all the time, *"How do I make a movie?" "How do I get my writings out there?" "How do I???"*

In answer to all of this and more, what you do have to do is, get your mind out of the gutter; if I can borrow that old saying. And, you have to make your reality a better, more positive, and more creative place. How do you do that? Answer, you do it. You stop all forms of outwardly focusing on anything that does not make your reality, and the reality of all those around you, better. You end the negativity. And, you focus on the creativity. You focus on the creating. You focus on the doing well. It can be anything! It can be working in your garden if that's what makes you happy.

For example, I know my father-in-law, (RIP), he used to love to create bonsai trees. All his neighbors would ask him to come to their garden and trim their trees for them. And, he happily did it. He refused all forms of payment, except for when he was working for Frank Sinatra. Where was paid quite handsomely. But, for his neighbors, he happily did it for free. Why? Because he loved that creative process. Meaning, creativity can be whatever you see it to be. But, the one thing that true creativity never is, is focusing your unresolved anger, your undefined Mind Junk, and you're unspecified need for embracing negativity anywhere in the external.

Be positive. Do good. Be creative. You want to live a good life? You want to achieve your dreams? That's the pathway.

*　　*　　*

26/Feb/2026 09:53 AM

Does anyone think that AI is not going to take over reality?

EVERYTHING ZEN

24/Feb/2026 04:30 PM

Kind of funny, I guess… I had just finished setting up a guitar I had just picked up, and I thought I'd take a few moments and kick back. So, I sat back and flipped on the TV and did a bit of channel surfing. I popped over to MTV Classic. Just as I did, the song, *Everything Zen,* by Bush started to play.

I guess it was kind of like a precursor premonition, or perhaps a projection, as I had recently been thinking about that song over the last couple of days. You know how it is when you get a song in the back of your mind and you think you really have got to play it. You remember how good it was, and you just want to hear it again. Though I hadn't got around to doing that yet, I was lucky enough to hear it and/or see it on the TV screen. Great song!

I totally remember the first time I heard that song. My lady and I were driving out of Monterey, heading down the coast back down to L.A. It was the afternoon, and that song came on the radio. But, you know how the radio is sometimes, as you're driving away from the source, the music starts to get all broken up. But, from the moment I heard that song, I was shook. I thought, what a great song. And though it faded in and out, I was really excited about it. Plus, also, I guess I was a little bit worried that I wasn't going to ever be able to hear it again, as this was long before the days of Shazam and stuff like that. So, I didn't know who the song was by. Luckily, however, it became a big hit.

You know, it's kind of like I say to people a lot of times, when they're either asking me questions or interviewing me or something like that. I tell them, you're asking the wrong questions.

The thing is, people always seem to have an answer. They have an answer for a question that hasn't been asked. And, if they do have a question, they've already made up their mind about what answer they expect. Thus, pretty much no answer you give them is going to be what they want to hear. This is especially the case with something like Zen. So many times, people ask me about my involvement with things like Zen. And, what does it mean to me?

When that occurs, I always respond to their question with a question. To their question, my question is, *"Tell me, what is Zen?"* What I do is to turn it around. Because everybody already has an idea about what they think they think about, but they never really know. They never really take the time to investigate what they believe. They just want to project their own opinion onto what other people believe. So, when they asked me about Zen, I ask them to define what they think Zen actually is. The responses I have received are, in some cases, pretty comical. I could list a whole long plethora of the answers I've received. But mostly, people just dodge the question because they don't have an actual, well thought-out answer. They just want me to answer it for them so they can like, dislike, praise, or criticize what I say.

But, think about it, isn't the ultimate truth of Zen is that there is no all-encompassing definition of Zen? Thus, for anybody, including myself, who tries to lay a definition onto it, inevitably, it's wrong.

How can there be a definition to something as abstract as Zen?

So, *"Everything Zen. I don't think so,"* as the lyrics from that song plainly state. I disagree, the ultimate truth of life, *"Everything is Zen."* There's no definition. There are just people attempting to try to find a definition. Because in the ultimate truth of our reality, nobody really knows anything. At most, they just believe they know. And, in that belief, they lose the true essence of anything that actually is. Because all they are doing is projecting belief, which is based upon nothing more than a speculation, perhaps predefined by some scripture composed by some person who did or did not actually exist thousands of years ago. At best, they are attempting to define something that can never truly be defined or even understand; namely: the completely abstract reality of life.

Thus, Everything is Zen. And, in Zen, there is No Definition.

SO MUCH HISTORY IS FORGOTTEN

24/Feb/2026 07:01 AM

I had a weird flash as I was sitting here reading over an article about this musician who had a passing relationship with a much younger actress a million years ago. He remembers it. She remembers it. Though they both remember what took place differently… Or, at least, they want the story to be told the way they want the story to be told… But, it happened, then it was gone. If they had not been celebrities, no one would even care. No one would be writing about it, or reading about it, all these years later.

Think about your own life. Think about what you have lived and whom you have lived it with. Think about it. For the most part, no one but you, (and them), even knows what took place. Once they are gone—once you are gone, all that was lived will be gone. Then what?

For some reason, after reading that article, the memory of one of my long-terms friends popped into my mind. He's dead now. So, the only one left who remembers what we lived is me.

I remember, but no one else knows. I've never told the stories to anyone. Why would I? No one has written an article about us. Why would they? So, when I'm gone, all that we lived will be gone.

His wife died before him. His daughter doesn't know about the stuff we did. She never asked me. His grandkids will never know. They don't even know who I am. All that was lived; gone. Then what?

You know, this is the case with all of our lives and our life experiences. We experience that something whatever with that whom-ever. It is lived. It may be remembered by those who lived it. But, no one lives forever. So, if it's not noteworthy enough to be written about, and then read about by others, it will be forgotten, meaning nothing to no one who is left alive. Then what?

So, here we are. This is your life. What have you lived? Who have you lived it with? How will what was lived be known to anyone but you? How will you, and what you lived, be remembered when you are no more?

And perhaps, the overreaching truth, as what you lived will be known to no one but you, it ultimately meant nothing at all on the universal grand scheme of reality.

* * *

23/Feb/2026 08:58 AM

If you don’t clean your house, all it does it remain dirty.

PLAYING IN THE BIG LEAGUES

23/Feb/2026 08:40 AM

I forever find it interesting how younger people seek the position of age. Whereas, the older a person gets, they tend to look back at their youth as somewhat of a glorious time. This being said, this never changes the fact, that a young person seemingly wants to dance in the world of adults.

Recently, it's been brought to my attention, that a young person in my extended family is dancing in a world inhabited by adults, the realm of Mansion Parties.

I don't follow him, but apparently on his Insta, he's always showing himself at these big mansion parties, up in the Hollywood Hills, and around the greater L.A. area. The thing is, this guy's only sixteen years old. So, that means, that there's no way that he has the financial ability to actually set these parties up. He claims, he's just making some bank on the side from promoting them. And, good for him. Obviously, he's an entrepreneur.

Within all of this, however, there's a very big issue, these parties are sketchy scenes. I mean, I'm not alien to that world, and I know what goes on at these events. …Especially here in L.A., depending on who's attending, there can be a lot of dastardly deeds taking place, as well as things like gang activity, tons of drugs, tons of sex, tons of suckering young people into a lifestyle that they do not possess the mental capacity to even comprehend. Thus, I'm worried!

There's nothing I can do. I'm not his father. But, even me being who I am, the free minded person, I would not let my child be doing that and/or living that lifestyle. Yet, his parents seemed to be fine with it. So, god bless him. Mostly, I hope the kids going to be okay.

It's kind of like I look back to my life. When I was that young man's age, sixteen, I too was hanging out with a much older crowd. I mean, I had been drawn to Eastern

Mysticism since my earliest memory. I've spoken about this in the past, but I was a latchkey kid, and one of the things I would do pretty much on a daily basis, is I would watch the show, *Yoga for Health,* presented by a man named Richard Hittleman, on the PBS networks. There, he would teach the various aspects of yoga, in association with teaching the postures, the breathing techniques, meditation, and things like that. Meaning, I was into that stuff really young. Add to that my involvement in the martial arts, beginning at the age of six, and Eastern Mysticism has always been an essential part of my life. And, has (obviously) remained that way to this day.

Then, when I turned sixteen, and got a car, I was able to truly immerse myself into that spiritual world. It was then that I had a close friend, who was also very drawn to Eastern Spirituality, and he and I would go out to all of the spiritual centers and spiritual events around L.A. and beyond. …Seeking deeper knowledge and all of that kind of mystical sort of stuff. We really wanted to live that lifestyle.

I was still going to Hollywood High School at that point in time, so I had to take care of my studies, as well. But, come the evenings, and certainly on the weekends, he and I would delve out into that world.

During that time period, I found things like the Sufi Order, and Swami Satchidananda's Integral Yoga Institute. My friend went off to university. And, though we stayed friends for a number of years after that, we eventually went our separate ways. Me, I never left that whole lifestyle, however.

While I was at high school, with any of my free time, you could find me associating with those people. The thing is, though my friend group was mostly in their early thirties, they weren't involved in things like doing drugs, partying, wild sex, and all of the kind of nonsense that goes on at those big mansion parties. They were all celibate. They were completely anti-drug. They were vegetarians. They were practitioners of the various spiritual disciplines. Thus, I was in a safe environment. Though I was a decade or more younger than all of these people, I was very protected.

I always remember the time when it was on my seventeenth birthday and I was helping with a yoga retreat that was going on up in the Santa Monica Mountains. One of the Swamis realized that it was my birthday.

…Birthdays have never been that big of a deal to me. But, as I have come to understand, they are a really big deal for some people. Thus, the swami packed all of the staff up into our cars, and they took me out for carrot cake at a local cafe. The crew was all a little shocked when they found out that I was only seventeen years old. I found all of their amazement kind of funny. But, in looking back, I see that I was really living a very unique lifestyle for somebody of that age. Anyway… Enough about me.

What I'm saying here is, a lot of young people, for whatever reason, find themselves living in the world of adults. Personally, I never felt any different from those people when I was coming up. I felt like I had become an adult many years before that point. But, unlike my family member, I grew up in a really, (for lack of a better term), violent urban environment. Thus, I feel like I was more readily prepared to enter the world of adulthood, then say my family member who has lived a very sheltered life up until this point.

The fact is, I worry about him. I don't know that he has the chops to deal with the kind of stuff that can go on when the shit hits the fan in that environment. And, doing what he's doing, it will.

So, what am I saying here? What I'm saying is we each find ourselves living the life that is presented to us. Yes, we each have our foundational understandings about reality. Yes, we each have our own personal understanding of the world in which we hope to inhabit. Yes, we each can seek out those levels of existence where we can hopefully find what we are looking for. The existence where we wish to exist. This being said, a lot of life is based on availability. It's based on the people that are around us. It's based on those who influence us, whether we want their influence in our lives or not.

Ultimately what I'm saying is, children become adults. There's nothing we can do to stop that. We can hope that they will live a good, happy, and prosperous life. And, reach the level of existence that they desire. But, there's a lot of obstacles in the way. And, if you let the people around you—if you let your family members walk down that dark road, once they reach that dark side, there's no one to blame but yourself if things turn bad. Hopefully, and I can only wish, that that will not happen to my family member. He's young. And, youth is a blessing. The sad truth is, however, most young people never realize this fact until it's too late. Then, all you are left with is what you are left with. From this, the rest of your life may be defined by nothing more than the necessity of Clean Up and regret.

* * *

20/Feb/2026 09:04 AM

You can only create with what you have to create with.

MINDFUL SPEAKING

20/Feb/2026 07:58 AM

Mindful Speaking involves pausing to consider the impact of your words before uttering them, recognizing that speech carries the power to create life or cause destruction. Rooted in the biblical principle that, *"Death and life are in the power of the tongue,"* Proverbs 18:21. Mindful Speaking emphasizes using Right Speech to heal, encourage, and build up rather than to tear down or destroy.

"Speaking Your Mind," is often associated with raw honesty, emotional transparency, or even your Right. However, from a Mindful Perspective, believing in this ideology is not entirely based upon Truth if Your Mind is currently filled with anger, pride, or misinformation. Meaning, if your heart is not in the right place, speaking your mind can cause harm.

Proverbs 10:19 *"Keeping your mouth closed is a sign of wisdom; too many words lead to sin."*

Ephesians 4:29 *"Only speak what is helpful for building others up according to their needs."*

Matthew 12:36 *"We will give an account for every careless word spoken on the day of judgment."*

Those are just a few biblical passages that may give you some ideas about the spiritual perspective of Mindful Speaking.

From a Buddhist perspective, Mindful Speaking, or Right Speech is an essential element of higher consciousness. It is understood that Mindful Speaking is the practice of consciously choosing words that are true, necessary, kind, and helpful. It involves pausing before speaking to examine intentions, avoiding gossip, lies, and harsh words in order to cultivate compassion, reduce suffering, and to foster harmony via the words you speak.

To dive a bit deeper: The Sanskrit term used for Mindful Speaking is, *"Samvrta Vānmaya,"* which refers to restrained or Thoughtful Speech. Another related term is, *"Samyak Vāk,"* meaning, *"Right Speech."* This term is commonly referenced in Buddhist teachings to indicate Mindful and Ethical Communication. It is part of the Eightfold Path emphasizing truthful, harmonious, gentle, and meaningful speech, rooted in awareness, *"Smriti"* and clear comprehension, *"Samprajanya."*

Buddhism, as a spiritual tradition, emphasizes Mindfulness in all aspects of life, including the way we communicate. Mindful Speaking is a fundamental component of the Eightfold Path, guiding practitioners to cultivate awareness and compassion in their interactions. To reiterate, this principle encourages individuals to be conscious of their words, ensuring that speech is truthful, beneficial, and harmonious.

At the heart of Mindful Speaking lies the intention to avoid causing harm. The Buddha taught that all words spoken should refrain from lying, divisiveness, harshness, judgement, and idle chatter. Instead, practitioners are encouraged to speak with honesty, kindness, and purpose. By doing so, communication becomes a vehicle for fostering understanding and peace rather than conflict or confusion.

Mindful Speaking requires a deep awareness of one's thoughts and emotions before expressing them. This practice involves pausing to reflect on whether the words you are about to speak are necessary, helpful, and delivered at the right time. Such mindfulness transforms conversations into opportunities for growth and connection, rather than occasions for judgment or misunderstanding.

Furthermore, Mindful Speaking is intimately connected to the cultivation of compassion. In Buddhism, compassion is not limited to actions but extends to language. By choosing words carefully and considering their impact, practitioners support the well-being of themselves and others. This approach helps create a supportive environment where people feel heard and respected.

In today's often polarized world, the teachings on Mindful Speaking are increasingly relevant. Practicing Right Speech can counteract negative communication patterns and promote harmony in families, friendships, workplaces, and communities. It encourages people to listen deeply, respond thoughtfully, and contribute positively to the collective dialogue, while never embracing any form of negativity.

Ultimately, Mindful Speaking is more than just a set of rules. Instead, it is a way of existing within a higher state of being—living in manner that reflects the values of Awareness, Compassion, and Ethical Conduct. By integrating these principles into your daily life, practitioners can transform their relationships and cultivate a more peaceful and understanding society.

So, ask yourself, how often do you Speak Mindfully? How often are you truly consciously aware of what you are saying and why? How often do you speak to hurt? Verses, how often do you speak to help? And, do you actually know or care about the difference?

Like I say all the time, the world begins with you. What world are you planning to create based upon what you say?

GO FUND ME ON INDIEGOGO

18/Feb/2026 09:15 AM

You know, there was a time when it was illegal, and fairly immoral, to offer to give a person a role in a film only after they paid you for that role. I don't know when, where, or why this process changed. But, look at all the films that are seeking financing on crowd funding platforms like GoFundMe and Indiegogo, and it goes on all the time.

I don't know if there's really anything wrong in that process. I mean, so many people come to Hollywood seeking the dream of being in a film. Then, they pay tons of money to get headshots, they pay to take acting classes, they dream of getting an agent, but none of that guarantees them a role in a film. The funding sites do, however. So???

I know, way back in the way back when, when Don Jackson and I were casting films all the time, we had these offices in North Hollywood, and we were just deluged with people coming at us all the time wanting a role in a film. Some felt they really deserved it. But, I won't get into that. At least not right now. Sometimes, before we had even decided if we were going to cast a person or not, they would ask, *"How much does it pay?"* Our (joking) response would always be, *"How much are you going to pay us to put you in a film?"*

The funding websites are an interesting tool. I know some people who have raised a lot of money to make their movie on them. I've also encountered a few who have set up a page just to get the money and run. Personally, I've put some money into people's films that I did not personally know and that was the last I heard from them. I've also put some financing into projects that did become very real. So, it's a crap shoot. …And, I've watched as some established filmmakers put up a page and got next to nothing? So, what is the formula?

People come at me sometimes, questioning why don't I put up a page to get money to finance another film like, *Max Hell Frog Warrior, Samurai Vampire Bikers from Hell, Roller Blade Seven,* and the like. But, I have long understood the paradox of *Zen Filmmaking.* Ask yourself, *"Would you give me any money to make a film?"* My guess is, probably not. And, if you would be willing to give me some money to make a film, would it be enough to actually make that movie?

...Sure, some of you may like to watch the films. Some of you may even make money by writings about and criticizing the films. But, are you willing to give me money to make the films?

I mean, authors have even written chapters in books about my film and me. Same with Don. So???

Speaking of Don... Don Jackson, my Zen Filmmaking Brother, was a very different person than I. He came from an era in filmmaking of that is what people did, seek out financing. Then, once you get it, you shoot the movie. I've never been about that, however. I've never asked anyone for a dime to shoot my films. I have worked with some people who have happily supplied their time, their talent, their locations, and stuff like that. But, that was a mutual creative effort. And, I was very thankful for their contribution.

But, getting back to Don, I'm sure he would have loved the crowd funding era, where people paid to be credited as a producer, a cast member, a whatever...

I don't know, it's an interesting ballgame. A game with only the most fluctuant of rules. Yeah, getting free money must be nice—money to make that film you want to make. Give a person a screen credit, give them a role in the film, sure whatever. Why not? But, who really has the money to make that difference—that money and is willing to give it to someone else? As established as I am, I really doubt anyone would flock to any crowd funding page I would set up. But, to all you people out there who have suggested it, thanks for thinking about me!

WHEN A RAINBOW IS GONE

17/Feb/2026 09:26 AM

I don't know about where you live, but don't you love it when you see a rainbow? At least here in L.A., they are fairly few and far between. So, when one pops up in the sky, it's just so enthralling. The problem is, however, rainbows don't last forever. They're here and then they're gone. I always find that sad. You're looking at it, loving it, studying it, hoping it will last forever, but then it fades away.

Life is a lot like that, don't you think? I mean, so much of the good stuff is here and then it's gone. Sometimes that good stuff lasts a while. Other times, it's only here just for a moment. Here, and then it's gone.

The thing about life is, we all want what we love to last forever. We want it to stay around. But, through time, technology, karma, or simply human innovation and/or destruction, it will be here and then it will be gone.

You know, I've had this TV system that I've loved for a lot of years. When it came around, well over ten years ago now, it was just so good. So good, compared to what came before. Just the way it was designed and set up and functioned and… It just worked. Thousands of stations, all easy to track and to find, On Demand, you name it…

Every now and then, I would have some problems with the system. But, I would call up and the tech on that far off distant shore would set it right again.

Last night, again, I had a problem. *"God damn it!"* It's always frustrating to deal with something you don't feel like dealing with when you are all chilled and laid back.

We call 'em up. They run through some tests. Have us do a few things. No go. They have to send us a new box. It'll be here in a day or two. Until then… Well…

The tech continues, *"Oh, by the way, we are changing our system. The old system is being phased out"* Then comes the spiel. *"You will pay less. You will say over a thousand dollars in the first years, and..."*

If I were a conspiracy theorist, I would think that they probably set up the whole problem with my system to get our attention and make us make the call. And, maybe that is true. We took the bait. We are changing with the change.

So, I don't know what is/what will come next??? Got to wait a day or so to get the new system setup via the email and the???

But, you know, it's just sad to see things go. Things that you loved, but they are no more.

Just like the beauty of that rainbow, here and then it is gone.

Just like the lyric in that great song from that fictional band of the 1960s, Max Frost and Troopers, *"Nothing Can Change the Shape of Things to Come."*

*   *   *

16/Feb/2026 07:15 AM

If the person you are trying to attack with an insult takes it as a compliment, you have lost the battle.

* * *

15/Feb/2026 08:23 AM

The more exaggerated your self-image, the more problems you will encounter in your life.

THE KRIS DERRIG LES PAUL

13/Feb/2026 09:14 AM

This is kind of a very personalized and specific blog posting. I just update the page I have on this site devoted to my friend Kris Derrig, RIP. I originally posted that page twenty years ago in 2006. As I just added some new info to it, I thought that the few of you, (who care), may find it interesting.

I have posted both the previous and the new writings here in this blog for your pleasure.

Kris Derrig

I have noticed that there has been a lot of discussion about the evolution of the Kris Derrig Les Paul on the Internet. Much of this discussion is speculation and incorrect. As such, I thought I would write a few words on the subject as I was an actual friend of Kris. I knew him when he was happy and healthy and I sadly watched him fade away into sickness and death.

For the record, Kris' name is sometimes spelled Chris in the media and on the Internet. But, this is incorrect.

The Kris Derrig Les Paul

The story of Kris' Les Paul creations, (in California), occurred when he was hired in the mid 1980s by my long-time friend, Jim Foote, (who is every bit the luthier that Kris was and, no, Jim is not dead as Slash mistakenly stated in his autobiography). At that time, customizing and creating custom guitars was a common order of business. Jim, who was then working on guitars for many of the top rock stars of the era, hired Kris to help him refinish and customize guitars. In fact, many superstar bands of the era, such as Ratt, Great White, Dokken, and Guns and Roses, commonly rehearsed at Jim's shop, the Music Works, which had a rehearsal studio set up in the back building. From this, many of the bands had much of their guitar work done at the Music Works in association with their rehearsals. Aside from the Les Paul Kris created for me he also refinished and customized a number of my guitars, as well.

Kris' Les Pauls have become somewhat legendary in the industry as he only made a few before his untimely passing, from lung cancer, at the age of thirty-two. Most notably, Slash plays one, as does Lenny Kravitz and Charlie Daniels. There are only about seven or eight other California made Kris Derrig Les Pauls out there that I am aware of. When he was making them at the Music Works he had more than one client who would further age the guitar, once it was created, and then sell it as an original 1958 Gibson Les Paul. So, some of his creation may never be found—as they are thought to be a true Gibson Les Paul. But, for the aficionado, if you look at the routing and the pickup cavities, Kris created them slightly different from the Gibsons of the late 1950s and there are a few other things that can be noticed by the trained eye. Jim Foote is the only person that I know of who can truly authenticate a Derrig Les Paul.

Side Note:

A little known fact about Kris is that, aside from being a luthier of guitars, he was also a hairstylist. He had been trained and practiced this craft when he lived in Atlanta. As such, when he moved to California and began working at the Music Works, he would periodically cut the hair of staff members, customers, and friends of the shop.

The 1960 Kris Derrig Les Paul

The history of the guitar he made for me began when Kris had some free time and began to create a new Les Paul to sell—as he was always in need of money. In association with making guitars and customizing others, he was busy converting a vintage Pontiac Tempest into a GTO. Each week he would go to the pick-a-part junk yard seeking parts for his automotive creation. One afternoon, at about four o'clock, he called me up. He had found a part he really needed. I forget what it was. But, he needed money fast. $950.00 to be exact. This is what he asked me to pay him for the Les Paul, though he normally charged in excess of $1,500.00. I went to the bank and gave him the money later that afternoon.

As it was still not complete, I wanted Kris to take the guitar in a slightly different direction from the other Les Pauls he had crated while at the Music Works. So, I brought him a set of, *"Patent Applied For,"* gold Grover tuning keys that I had laying around, a set of Gibson PAFs with gold posts and pickup covers, and a vintage gold Gibson ABR bridge. He finished the guitar the next week, grabbing some of the remaining needed parts from the wall of the Music Works, which annoyed Jim. *"Someone has to pay me for those parts!"* I guess it was Kris, because it wasn't me.

Kris made the guitar with the inspiration of the 1960 Gibson Les Paul. The neck is thin like a 1960 Les Paul and the Serial Number reflects 1960 Gibson. All of Kris' other Les Pauls are based on the late 1950s Les Pauls, which makes the one he created for me a very unique piece of Kris' heritage.

When Kris created the guitar he tried to match the sunburst of the 1960 Les Paul that he saw in books, but the color was somewhat off. I knew this because I owned an actual 1960 Gibson Les Paul. In the early 1990s, long after Kris' passing, I had Jim Foote refinish it for me. He did a great job and matched 1960 Gibson coloring perfectly. He then let it hang in his shop for a couple of years, as he was distracted by other projects. Though I would have preferred to have it put together, the time did sun-age the finish perfectly.

And, that is the story of the creation of the 1960 Kris Derrig Les Paul.

Sadly, Kris passed away before he ever knew that the guitars he created were to become the legendary instruments that they became.

Mostly, Kris was a great guy and a close friend. He has been missed since his passing over twenty years ago. He was one of those unique individuals who left this place we call LIFE way too soon.

Follow Up:

I initially wrote this piece twenty years ago, in 2006. It's now 2026 and the interest in Kris Derrig and the guitars he created has remained a strong topic.

I thought I would take a moment and speak just a little bit more about Kris and his life here in L.A. for those of you who have developed an interest.

When he first moved to the Los Angeles area, he was sharing an apartment with a roommate in Hermosa Beach. This is where he lived when he first began working for Jim Foote at his store, The Music Works. The original Music Work location was situated on Artesia Blvd., in Redondo Beach.

Kris came to work for Jim during a time when many musicians, including myself, were having all kind of modifications and refinishing work done to their guitars. Thus, Jim was deluged with work.

At that time, Jim had his main assistant, Ken Hitsman by his side. Plus, there were a couple of other temporary workers who came and then went. When Kris arrived, he told Jim about his expertise and the history of how he had created his Les Pauls. Jim hired him.

From the moment Kris arrived, he showed his prowess as a master luthier and guitar technician. He did a lot of work on a lot of guitars in association with creating a few of his Les Pauls.

As mentioned in the previous discourse, he did some fantastic work on reworking and refinishing some of my guitars. Plus, he worked on guitars for some of the top players of the era. Plus, a lot of others.

Once he was established at the Music Works, he and Ken drove across the country to where he had been previously living in Atlanta. Once there, the pair gathered his possession and brough them to California.

As time went on, and his relationship with Jim grew closer, Kris was not only restoring and converting the Tempest into a GTO, but he had also purchased an Airstream trailer which he was restoring. Upon buying that trailer, he parked it in the rear of the Music Works, and moved in. This was his new home. This is where he lived until his sickness took hold of him.

The thing about this trailer was, it was in barebones condition. It was basically gutted and there was no insolation or heating or anything like that. As Kris began to show signs of his illness, I could not help but wonder did his living condition aid in its rapid approach. By the time he went to a doctor, his condition was already in an advanced stage.

Kris returned to his hometown for a period of time to receive treatment. When his condition seemingly went into remission, and as soon as he was able, he returned to California. Once here, he stayed with Jim, and his then wife Jill, at their apartment in Beverly Hills.

I remember speaking to Kris one day, and he lamented how the chemo had made him lose all of his very long locks of hair. I made the joke, no matter how many times you cut it, your hair will always grow back.

Sadly, his condition did not remain in remission for very long. Shortly thereafter, he succumb to his cancer in May of 1987.

For those of us who knew him, we understand that he was a super nice, very reserved, master craftsman. Just a good guy! For everyone else, he left the world with a few guitars that have help to shape musical history long after his passing.

I trust this will provide you with a bit more information about the life and times of Kris Derrig.

KILLING YOURSELF TO LIVE

12/Feb/2026 08:00 AM

It seems that whenever a celebrity passes away, the fragileness of life is really brought into focus. We are here, and then we are gone. That's just the reality of life. But, I think most people don't really think about the wider implications of what will happen when they pass away.

Yesterday, the actor James Van Der Beek passed away due to colorectal cancer. Apparently, that's the current leading cause of death of men under fifty, at least here in the United States. It's sad, really. He was only forty-eight years old. And, he leaves behind his wife and six children.

Forty-eight, that's the same age my father died when I was ten years old. So yes, people can die. Die, much earlier in their life than is expected.

One of the facts that has been widely overlooked, with the passing of Van Der Beek, is that Bud Cort, of Harold and Maude fame, he died yesterday, as well. But, he was seventy-seven, so there's something a bit more expected when somebody passes away at that age. That doesn't make it any easier for the loved ones, but it just is somehow more acknowledged.

A lot of people die young. My friend, Kris Derrig, who made the legendary Les Paul that Slash played on, Appetite for Destruction, he died when he was only thirty-two. Complications from lung cancer. Good guy. Sorely missed. A man, Mark Williams, who worked with Don Jackson and I on, *The Roller Blade Seven,* he died when he was only thirty-eight. Complications from prostate cancer. He and I were born the same year. And, as mentioned, my father died at forty-eight from a massive heart attack. He was at work, as manager of the Los Angeles Forum, when he apparently just keeled over and died.

The thing is, life is life, and then it's over. When it comes at you slowly, like say, dying from cancer, there is perhaps some more time for mental preparation. But, that doesn't make it any easier. And, I'm not sure if that is a good or a bad thing.

I was reading this morning that Van Der Beek's family has set up a Go Fund Me page, to take care of expenses. Because, obviously, the actor hasn't been working for quite a while since he's been diagnosed.

What will become of that family? I don't know? I know it was a massive shock to my life when my father died at forty-eight, and the things that happened after that really did a lot of destructive stuff to me as a human being, and the overall evolution of my life. But, here I still am, for whatever it's worth.

I know this guy, he's a few years older than me, and he recently just had another child. Now, this guy is in great shape and he looks very good for his age. But, the fact of the fact is, by the time that kid is ten years old, he's going to be eighty. What ten year old wants an eighty year old as a father. Plus, if he's lucky enough to live that long, when his kid turns twenty, he's going to be ninety. You know, it's just one of those things, just because you can, doesn't mean that you should.

From the metaphysical perspective, we all know we're going to die at some point. But, all we can live is what we live. This is where the complications of life arise. This is where karma arises. This is where religion arises. This is where the promise of heaven and/or hell, paradise with Allah, Nirvana with the Buddha, and all of that kind of stuff comes from. There's all of these promises made about what we're going to meet when we die, based upon who we are while we are living. This is why all religions propagate the fact that you really need to be as good as possible, because goodness is the only way you can reach that higher state of being after you've passed away.

But, I'm sorry, all that means nothing! It's like, the awards they give to people after they've passed away. What does it mean? They're dead! If you want to let someone know they're loved, you've got to reach out to them while they are alive.

No matter what they believed, no matter what you believe, there is one simple reality, dead is dead, and then it's just the living who are left to deal with what you have left behind.

So, here's the question, what are you leaving behind? If you were to pass away today, what would be left in your wake?

A sidebar here… You know, when I was twenty-one, I was riding my motorcycle, and a car hit me, and literally almost killed me. For the first few days, they thought I was nothing but dead. Luckily, some neurologist drilled into my skull, stopped the bleeding in my brain, and lifted my skull off of my frontal lobe. I was banged up as all fuck, and I was never the same. Yet, I was alive. And I'm here to this day. Meaning, you can die at any moment. Are you, your life, and your karma ready to meet that ultimate stage? Because that's what it is, as we're all going to go there. And really, nobody knows what's going to happen once you get there. It's all philosophic bullshit. So again, are you ready to meet your maker, as the old saying goes. If you're not, you should really stop screwing around and get your life in order. Because when you're dead, you're dead and it can happen at any moment.

TWO SIDES OF THE NARRATIVE

11/Feb/2026 07:08 AM

The Sanskrit word for truth is, *"Satya."* In Hinduism and Buddhism, Satya is an integral part of all reality. But ultimately, what is the truth?

I mean, just think about it. How important is truth to you? I believe for most of us, truth is a very important element of our life. We hope the other people we encounter in life are truthful and honest to us in all of our life-dealings. In fact, for most of us, we, at least initially, believe what people say to us. We trust what they say to be the truth.

But, think about how many people lie. Think how many people intentionally alter the truth. Think about how many put their own spin on whatever reality they have lived. And, they do this, based simply upon how they want the story to be told, how they wish to be perceived, what they hope to gain from that someone else, and how they want their life and their life-history to be illustrated. Have you ever told a lie?

Have you ever been in one of those situations where one person is telling the story about a life event that took place? You listen. You hear. And, you believe what they say to be true. Then, perhaps sometime later, you hear the same story told by another individual who lived that same life event and it is explained in a totally different way. The pathway to the end, and the facts that lead to their conclusions about the situation are depicted in a completely different manner than that which was explained to you by the other person. Then what? Who is telling the truth?

Maybe you have found yourself in one of those situations. You lived a life event with that someone else. You thought you experienced the same thing. But, when they told the story through their eyes it was something completely different from the way you remembered it to be. So, here's the question, who is telling the truth?

One would think that life should be simple, and the truth should be the truth. And, in many cases that is the fact. The truth is the truth, but it is only altered by the person who wishes it to be painted in a different way.

But, then there is this whole other reality. That reality is, personal perception. What is person perception? The way an individual perceives, judges, and ultimately concludes their reality.

Is your reality the truth? Is the way you perceive your reality based upon the truth? Or, is it altered by the way you desire it to be viewed?

The simple fact is, you can tell the truth. Or, you cannot. The truth is the truth is the truth is the truth. It is *satya.* Or, you can alter it by the way you want it to be understood.

Ultimately, as you pass through your life, you will encounter those who try to tell the truth in the most truthful manner possible. But, no matter how truthful they perceive themselves to be, there is no one that is not dominated by their own mind. And, though they may be telling the truth from their own perspective, that is all it is, their own perspective.

Remember that whenever you ever listen to anyone saying anything to you.

The truth is, at best, defined by the mind of the person who is telling it.

* * *

10/Feb/2026 08:55 AM

If you were to lose something everyday, how long would it take for you to have nothing?

*   *   *

10/Feb/2026 08:55 AM

If you have to tell someone that you are enlightened that means that you are not.

HOW MUCH IT COSTS DOES NOT DEFINE WHO YOU ARE

10/Feb/2026 07:36 AM

Way back in the way back when, my local Trader Joe's used to sell this chianti that was very-very good. It was the kind of bottle that had the bamboo wrapping around the bottom of it.

I don't know… There's just something cool about that. You don't see it too much anymore. But, it did/does provide the whole drinking wine experience with a vibe.

This was back when I lived on the Esplanade in Redondo and I would hit up the Trader Joe's in the Village.

Sometimes, when I had a little money in the bank, I would buy that wine by the case. Mostly, I would just stop in and pick up a couple of bottles of it a few times a week in association with whatever I was buying for dinner.

FYI: I'm not one of those people who buys food way in advance, and stocks up their refrigerator, like most people do. Pretty much I only buy food one day at a time. Keep it fresh and all…

For whatever reason, it seemed like there was frequently this one girl working the cash registered in the evenings when I would be checking out. I didn't think too much about it. That was just the way it was.

One night, however, she made the comment to me, *"You always buy cheap wine."* What??? That statement kind of hit me hard, in one of those weird sort of ways. I mean, here I am, a guy who is not averse to spending a hundred dollars, or much more, on a bottle of wine while dining out or elsewhere. But, I only bough this wine because it was, as stated, really good.

Now, I've spoken about this in the past, but the price of a bottle of wine in no way guarantees that it will possess a grand flavor. I mean, I've been given some very expensive bottles of wine as a gift and after a sip or two, as they were so bad, I just poured them done the sink. Anyway…

I thought that was kind of an underhanded comment. Kind of like an insult. Why, she said that, I have no idea? What she meant by it, is a question. But, the way it came out, really put me off and set me to thinking. One thought was, *"Fuck you. Is that the way you are supposed to speak to your customers?"* The other was, *"It's really sad that you need to make yourself feel better about yourself by subtly attacking someone else's choices."* And then, *"I guess you only take note of me buying the chianti and not the so many other bottles of wine I have purchased from this store, over the years, that were far more expensive. But, that did not make them taste any better."*

I guess if they had Yelp back then I could have written a negative review. ☺

For the most part, I've had nothing but nice experiences with the people I've met that worked at Trader Joe's. I've even become friends with some of them. But…

I imagine we've all encountered situations like that at some point in our life. Someone wanting to feel like something more by putting us down. Maybe you have even done that?

I believe the key element through all of this is, in life, people have two ways to encounter their destiny. One, they can accept it and come to love it. Or two, if they do not like it, they can devise a method to change it. But, by trying to gain standing by speaking down to or about someone else, that style of action achieves nothing and all that those words do is to cause a person, like me in this situation, to remember you in a negative manner.

Whatever happened to that girl? I have no idea. Eventually she was, at least at that Trader Joe's, no longer there. Did she find happiness in a place where she did not have to diminish the likes of someone else? I will never know. What I do know is, if you must criticize or diminish the like(s) and/or the life and lifestyle of anyone else, just to make yourself feel better about yourself, you are walking the wrong life path.

TOO MUCH MELODRAMA

09/Feb/2026 08:14 AM

Have you ever met one of those people that just thrives on melodrama? Maybe you are one of them?

Life is life, and it is going along as life goes along, but then a person who bases their life on melodrama come into your sphere of existence and do to their mindset and their uncontrolled ideology they forever stir the pot and make everything into a big something. A something that it should never have become.

I know I've encountered people like that. And, people like that just suck you into the whatever it is they are melodrama-ing about.

I guess there's just that something in the adrenalizing of the all and the everything that becomes such a drug that some people fall into that pattern. And, in some cases, they can never pull themselves out. They just keep the melodrama existing and growing and expanding and affecting the lives of all those they encounter.

It's sad, really. Because most people don't want to live their life at that level. They simply want to exist and not encounter conflict. But, put one of those people into the mix and BOOM chaos is invoked and it explodes in all directions.

From my own life experience(s), I know I've had people throw melodrama into the mix of my life. In some cases, from out of nowhere. There have been moments in my life where everything is fine, then that someone, for some reason, motivated by whatever misguided whatever they have chosen to conjure up, decided to blow up my life. Did it give them a sense of empowerment? Maybe? Did they feel they had the right to do what they did? Possibly. Were they simply acting out of some misguided sense of all-knowing percussion and domination? Perhaps. But, what they did was to set a chain of events into motion that hurt my existence and myself and those I care about around me. So, ask yourself, what is the karma in that? And perhaps, even more importantly, ask yourself, have you ever done that to anybody?

I know in a couple of cases, after doing what they did to me, I observed as they got hit with some really hardcore something. Did they look to themselves as the causation factor? Nope. They simply cried, *"Woe is me."* Meaning, that people who operate at this level of life are so unaware of who they are, what they are, and how what they are doing is interacting with the greater cosmos as a whole, that they are too blind to understand that what they are doing not only affects the life of the person they are trying to focus on, but what they are doing ultimately affects their own life, as well.

This is really an important thing to think about as you pass through your life. What are you creating in the life of others, based upon your own motivational motivation? Motivation, whether consciously known or not. What is what you are doing, doing to their life of others? What is it doing to your own life? And, how much of it is based upon nothing more than your own melodrama?

Now, I get it… The people who operate on this level are generally so out of touch with their own karmic reality that they do not possess the true ability to study the actuality of their actions. Or, maybe they feel they have the right to do whatever it is they choose to do? I don't know? Or, maybe they are just don't care? That's a possibility. Or, maybe they intentionally want to fuck up the someone and the everything as much as possible? Some people are like that.

The thing is, people who do these things are operating in a very negative life space. I can say, stay away from them. But, in some cases, these people attack from afar, and there is nothing that you can do about their chaotic aggression. So, then what?

The fact is, there is no one answer. I can say, don't get sucked into it. Or, don't let it bother you. Or, they will get theirs. But, all of that means nothing when you are in the middle of melodramatic chaos.

All of this ultimately comes down to the questions, who are you? What are you? Are you a creator of melodrama? Or, are you a creator of goodness and peace? Really, who are you?

Study your own life. Truly look deep. What melodrama have you created in your own existence? What melodrama have you created in the life of that someone else? Now, ask yourself, what did the creation of that melodrama prove? Did it make anything better for anyone?

Ultimately, if you are honest with yourself, your answer will be, no it did not. It did not make anything any better.

So, here's the test, is what you are about to do going to cause melodrama in the life of yourself or anyone else? If it is, don't do it.

Is what someone else is doing creating that chaotic something? …Someone that you do or do not know. If they are, stay as far away from them as possible. And, never allow yourself to get sucked in.

Life melodrama is never a good thing. If you're creating it, stop it! If you've done it to others, undo it!

The ultimate goal is to live a life of peace and caring and giving. Never embrace the melodrama.

STUBBY SHAW AND THE TROJAN BARREL

07/Feb/2026 02:17 PM

After (again) reading over the bio on myself at Grokipedia, that I showed you in the last blog, I noticed that they mentioned, *"Publicly available information on his family background is limited. His father served in the military during World War II and earned a black belt in jujitsu."* This got me to thinking…

I guess I've never spoken too much about my parents or what they did in this blog or elsewhere, and no one, in interviews, ever really asked me about them. I guess there was never any real reason to do so. …That's just the way it has been.

Back in 2021, this USC historian did a piece on my father, and to a lessor degree my grandmother. He posted it on his blog, *"Inside USC with Scott Wolf."* It's really a good piece on my father, and it's a great blog as it provides a lot of his other research on USC people and history. I reposted the piece about my father here in this blog. It's still up with the title, *"It Doesn't Really Matter to Anyone but Me."* But, I think I may change that.

Maybe because I didn't mention my father's name in the title, or better put, at least in terms of the USC article, his nickname, none of the AIs out there are grabbing it. And, as there is no reference to me in the man's article, no one knows that we were related. Anyway, for the whatever it's worth, I'm going to repost that blog here and now. I'm going to also leave the little bit I originally wrote pre the man's article intact, as well; just for the whatever of the whatever...

Anyway, here's a little bit about my family background for any of you (and all the AI out there) who may have cared.

It Doesn't Really Matter to Anyone but Me

Several years ago, I made a statement and titled a blog, something to the effect, *"No One Remembers My Father But Me."* This statement was based in the fact that he passed on in 1968, I was an only child, all the family quickly dispersed after his passing, and I now know none of them, etc… I'm the last man standing. I held on to this belief until earlier this year when I came upon a blog dedicated to the history of USC, (University of Southern California), where the historian, who runs that blog, began to speak of my father and even my grandmother. WOW! That was a surprise. Then, a couple of other people chimed in and spoke of their memories of my father and the USC themed restaurant he owned way back when.

I imagine the historian is not that old and did not personally know my father. From his entries, it reads more like a historical quest for the people that shaped the USC lifestyle. Which is very cool. He must love USC. And, he's doing what no one else seems to be doing. But, for those people who actually interacted with my father, they must be very-very old by now.

The point being, I guess I was wrong. I'm not the only person who remembers my father.

All this being said, and the point of this piece's being, does any of this really matter to anyone but me? For those reading that man's blog, do they really care about my father? Sure, a mention of a man, and there are a lot of USC orientated historical figures mentioned in the man's research and writings, may make a person marginally intrigued. But, do they truly care? I don't think so.

This is the important thing to keep in mind as you pass through your life. Who really cares? Who cares about you? Who cares about what you care about? And, who will care about what you provided to the world, ten, twenty, or a hundred years down the line?

Most people exist in a space of selfishness. They only care about who and what they care about until they care about them/it no more. So truly, what will your life have meant when you are no more?

Below, I am going to copy and paste the writings the man has collected about my father in the order they were published. Don't worry, it's not that much stuff. I don't know, you may find it interesting??? Or maybe, it may just kill a moment or two of your Life Time if you don't have anything better to do. There's also a link to the man's blog. It's really a big one.

Anyway… Think about it… Who cares about you? Who cares about me? And, who cares about what you and I care about?

May 14, 2021

Does anyone remember Stubby Shaw?

He opened the Trojan Barrel bar in 1955 that eventually turned into Julie's Trojan Barrel in 1975, which was not to be confused with Julie's Restaurant on Flower St., which was opened in 1941. Those were owned by the legendary Julie Kohl.

But back to Shaw. He was a fixture to students in the 1950's and would sponsor intramural basketball teams that featured actual players like Jim Kaufman and Danny Rogers.

If Shaw was well known, so was his mother. Known to dental students as *"Mrs. Shaw,"* she was fixture at the dental school from 1931-62.

Mrs. Shaw (born Maude Frances Mashburn) worked with more than 3,000 dental students, the *"little white haired lady who signs (the) state board examination card indicating the culmination of formal dental training."*

Some would say this was a time period back when USC was known for having family atmosphere.

May 17, 2021

As so often happens when I write about USC history, after initially writing about a subject I learn more through readers and more research.

I asked if anyone remembered Stubby Shaw on Friday.

In 1955, Shaw opened *"Stubby's Trojan Barrel"* bar near USC. Many students simply called it *"Stubby's."*

Around 1965, it was purchased by Marlin and Mike McKeever. I'm not sure how long the McKeevers owned it, but in 1975 Julie Kohl purchased the bar and it became *"Julie's Trojan Barrel."*

"It was so dark, you couldn't see yourself," a reader who went to Stubby's in the 1950's told me.

Frankly, that's what I remember about going there when it was *"Julie's Trojan Barrel."* You could walk in for lunch and it was like walking into a cave.

A USC alum told me Friday he thought Shaw might have played for the L.A. Dons football team.

Over the weekend, I came across a photo from 1956-57 of Stubby's and on the far right is Shaw himself. Now you know why he was nicknamed Stubby.

July 30, 2021

And now for some history:

I heard a great story this week regarding Stubby Shaw, the owner of Stubby's Trojan Barrel, which later became Julie's Trojan Barrel.

In the early 1960's, an underage USC student walked in Stubby's.

"Whaddya drinking?" Stubby growled.

"I'll . . . have . . . a . . . water," the terrified student said. *"Water?"* Stubby said incredulously. *"If you want water, go to the Union 76 across the street. We drink beer in here."*

August 6, 2021

Here's another story on Stubby Shaw, who owned Stubby's Trojan Barrel, which later became Julie's Trojan Barrel.

"He had a real red face, he was always red," said a USC student from the early 1960's. *"He looked like a football player. I think he played for the L.A. Dons (the first pro team to play in the Coliseum from 1946-49). He really kept the place in order. The McKeever twins really wanted the place and eventually bought it from him."*

January 21, 2022

Here's a 1948 photo of a game between the L.A. Dons and Cleveland Browns. The Browns defensive player who ran into the goal post, Tony Adamle, is the father of former NFL player/NBC Sports announcer Mike Adamle.

Remember, the infamous Stubby Shaw played for the L.A. Dons.

But the main reason I ran this photo is the clean look of the Peristyle, free of all the bric-a-brac USC stuck there over the years.

April 15, 2022

And now for some history:

Stubby Shaw (right) at his bar on Figueroa and 37th street circa 1956-57.

One of the things I love writing about USC history is the way I stumble across more stories. I've written before about Stubby Shaw, who opened *"Stubby's Trojan Barrel"* in 1955. Around 1965, Shaw sold it to Marlin and Mike McKeever and in 1975 it was bought by Julie Kohl and became *"Julie's Trojan Barrel."*

This story came from an alum:

One night, in the early 1960's, a customer kept giving Shaw a hard time, making rude comments and threats. As the customer prepared to leave, Shaw ran out the back entrance of the bar and went to the front entrance, which had two swinging doors like a Western saloon in the movies.

When the customer exited, Shaw punched him so hard, he flew back into the bar through the swinging doors. *"Don't ever come back here again!"* Shaw growled.

If you look at the photo, I'm not sure why anyone would antagonize Shaw.

April 22, 2022

Last week I told the story of Stubby Shaw punching one of his customers through the swinging doors at his bar on Figueroa and 37th street. He was also a fixture to students in the 1950's and would sponsor intramural basketball teams that featured actual players like Jim Kaufman and Danny Rogers.

In conclusion… As a small child, I spend many-many hours at the Trojan Barrel. I've told some of the stories I lived in novels and in other writings. As referenced in that blog by that onlooker, I too witnessed my father punch more than one guy in the face. It was a college bar okay… It could be a ruckus place, especially after a game. Though he wouldn't take any shit, mostly my father was a good guy. He liked to hang out behind the bar, always with a cigarette in his hand, pulling beers from the beer tap, and talking to his patrons. I drank my first beer there at a very young age. Plus, I have a photo of me, pulling beer, when I could not yet even walk. So, as all fathers are, and in some cases their jobs, that place was a formative part of my early existence.

But again, back to the truth of the truth… Does any of that matter to you? Probably not. So, when you and I are gone, who will care about what you and I cared about? Keep that in mind.

PS: Just for the record, I didn't go to USC. I paid my own way through college, and I couldn't afford a school like that. Though, in reading this man's blog, I guess I wish I could have.

GROKIPEDIA

06/Feb/2026 02:40 PM

Okay… This may turn out to be a bit of a lengthy piece. A lengthy piece that I did not write the most of…

Where to start???

First of all, as those of you who read this blog understand, I have never been a fan of Wikipedia. Sure, I use it from time to time for some quick info. But, since its inception, it has always been way too opinion-based to be a site that provides hard and true facts consistently. Anybody can edit on the site. With that, comes a lot of people who point a subject or a person's bio in a very specific direction; be it positive or negative.

I guess, I'm out of the loop, but someone just let me know about my bio on a new AI powered site launched by X, Grokipedia. All good, I love AI. On that site, so I was shown, was a bio of yours truly and one of DGJ. And, also some stuff about some of our films like *The Roller Blade Seven, Max Hell Frog Warrior,* and *Guns of El Chupacabra* and my films *Vampire Blvd.* and *Undercover X.*

I read the one on DGJ first and thought it was pretty good. I was initially just going to post that one for your reading pleasure. Then, I read the one about me. Interesting…

The thing that I find compelling about this site is that the articles read like they were written by a person doing a research paper, complete with references. Very human, yet factual.

So, I don't know??? Maybe times are changing and a new internet-able source of information has been born, Grokipedia. And, that's a good thing.

So, here they are, first the DGJ bio and then mine. I also provide links at the end. Not perfect, but pretty good…

Donald G. Jackson

Donald G. Jackson was an American independent filmmaker known for his low-budget cult films such as *Roller Blade* and *Hell Comes to Frogtown,* and for developing a distinctive *"Zen filmmaking"* approach—often in collaboration with Scott Shaw—that emphasized spontaneous creativity, location energy, and complete artistic control instead of traditional scripts or rigid structures. He frequently handled multiple key roles on his productions—including producer, director, writer, editor, and cinematographer—allowing him to maintain independence in the often-constrained world of low-budget cinema. His work in action, science fiction, and exploitation genres earned him a dedicated following among fans of unconventional and maverick independent films. Born on April 24, 1943, in Tremont, Mississippi, Jackson grew up in Adrian, Michigan, where he developed early interests in film, comic books, classic serials, and music. After moving to Los Angeles in 1981, he pursued his career in earnest, transitioning from early projects and industry work—including additional photography on films such as *The Terminator*—to creating his own distinctive body of work. His self-described Zen philosophy shaped many of his best-known productions, which often relied on improvisation and the unique energy of casts and locations rather than conventional narrative planning. Jackson remained active in filmmaking until the end of his life, battling leukemia after his 1995 diagnosis and continuing to produce and direct despite health challenges. He died on October 20, 2003, at age 60 at UCLA Medical Center in Los Angeles. His legacy endures through his pioneering role in independent cinema and the preservation of his films by collaborators.

Early life

Background and upbringing

Donald G. Jackson was born on April 24, 1943, in Tremont, Mississippi. He grew up in Adrian, Michigan, where he developed early interests in film, comic books, classic serials, and music. He relocated to Los Angeles in 1981 to pursue his film career. Limited details are available about his family background or childhood experiences in public sources.

Film career

Entry into filmmaking and early documentaries

Donald G. Jackson's interest in filmmaking emerged during his teenage years in Michigan, when he filmed local high school football games on 16 mm with a Bolex camera after being asked to fill in for an ill employer, capturing intimate footage from the middle of the field that marked the start of his *"no-rules"* approach to cinema. This early experience sparked a passion for the medium, further fueled by his viewing of *The Texas Chainsaw Massacre,* which convinced him that independent filmmakers could create distinctive work with an audience waiting. In the mid-to-late 1970s, Jackson completed his first feature, the horror parody *The Demon Lover,* co-directed with Jerry Younkins and financed through personal loans on his car and house after promised funding from Younkins failed to materialize; Jackson later expressed regret over the project due to its conflict with his Christian beliefs. Concurrently, he spent years shooting professional wrestling matches across the Midwest using 8 mm, Super 8, and 16 mm cameras, drawn to the sport since childhood and building a substantial archive of ringside material. This wrestling footage became the foundation for Jackson's early documentary efforts, particularly *I Like to Hurt People,* which originated in the mid-1970s as a planned horror film titled Ringside in Hell before shifting to a documentary format when consistent wrestler participation proved difficult. As director and producer, Jackson gained exceptional access to Detroit's Big Time Wrestling promotion through Ed Farhat (The Sheik), who permitted extensive filming of live matches and introduced him to key performers, resulting in footage featuring wrestlers including André the Giant, Abdullah the Butcher, and others in raw, unfiltered ring action. The project remained unfinished until the mid-1980s, when Jackson sold the material to New World Pictures, which funded additional staged scenes in 1984 to frame the documentary with a loose narrative around stopping The Sheik and released the completed film in 1985 on video and laserdisc. The distribution deal provided financial support and enabled Jackson to secure work as an assistant camera operator at New World Pictures and pursue further filmmaking opportunities in Los Angeles.

Breakthrough in narrative features

Donald G. Jackson gained recognition in independent cinema with the cult martial arts films *The Roller Blade Seven* (1991) and *Return of the Roller Blade Seven* (1993), which he directed, co-wrote, and co-produced in collaboration with Scott Shaw. These low-budget independent productions, completed in early 1992 and premiered at the American Film Market that year, followed a sword-wielding samurai on a rescue mission in a futuristic setting and were distributed direct-to-video, often through re-edited versions that reached international markets. They remain signature works in his oeuvre for their distinctive action-oriented approach within the constraints of minimal resources. In 1996, he directed and acted in Rollergator, a low-budget action film centered on a wisecracking alligator and a teenage girl on rollerblades evading pursuers. Throughout the late 1980s and early 1990s, Jackson's narrative output adhered to low-budget production methods and direct-to-video distribution patterns prevalent in exploitation, sci-fi, and action genres, allowing him to sustain prolific output in independent filmmaking.

Key collaborations and recurring partnerships

Donald G. Jackson developed his most significant and recurring professional partnership with filmmaker, actor, and writer Scott Shaw, with whom he collaborated extensively on low-budget independent films. Their work together spanned multiple projects, where they frequently shared credits in directing, writing, producing, and acting roles, creating a close creative alliance that lasted for years. This collaboration was particularly prominent in the *"Roller Blade"* series, including *"The Roller Blade Seven"* (1991) and *"Return of the Roller Blade Seven"* (1993), as well as other titles such as *"Guns of El Chupacabra"* (1997) and *"Armageddon Boulevard."* In these productions, Jackson typically handled directing duties while Shaw contributed as producer, co-writer, and lead actor, resulting in a distinctive style of spontaneous, action-oriented cinema. Their joint efforts also led to the formulation and promotion of *Zen Filmmaking,* an approach emphasizing intuition and minimal pre-planning in low-budget productions. Jackson also worked repeatedly with certain actors who appeared across his projects, including those made with Shaw. Joe Estevez featured in several films, becoming a familiar presence in their shared output after being introduced through their collaborations. Other performers, such as Don Stroud, also recurred in these circles of low-budget action and cult films. While Jackson had associations with other filmmakers like Fred Olen Ray, the partnership with Shaw stood out as the most sustained and multifaceted.

Development of Zen Filmmaking

Donald G. Jackson co-developed the approach known as *Zen Filmmaking* in collaboration with Scott Shaw beginning in 1991 during the production of *The Roller Blade*

Seven. The method emerged when the filmmakers abandoned a conventional screenplay after initial shooting proved disappointing, choosing instead to improvise the story spontaneously and shoot in the moment, which led Shaw to describe the process as *"Zen"* and coin the term *"Zen Filmmaking."* Jackson endorsed this shift, sharing the view that "*all the stories have already been told"* and that low-budget filmmaking should prioritize spontaneous artistic creativity over re-enacting pre-written narratives. The primary premise of *Zen Filmmaking* is that no screenplay is used in the creation of a film, freeing the process from a fixed mindset and allowing immediate inspiration to guide every aspect of production. This approach emphasizes improvisation, in-the-moment decision-making, and organic storytelling in which the narrative evolves naturally through cast and crew interactions rather than predetermined structure. Core principles include making unpredicted situations work to advantage, utilizing natural locations without artificial sets, prioritizing spontaneous action over elaborate planning, and ensuring the storyline does not dominate artistic vision. The philosophy further holds that *Zen Filmmaking* is a spontaneous process that embraces unpredictability and presence in the moment, with no fixed rules and an acceptance that all outcomes are perfect when nothing is rigidly desired. *Zen Filmmaking* focuses on the process of creation over the final product, viewing filmmaking as a meditative practice aimed at capturing *"cinematic enlightenment"* through unrestricted freedom and the inspiration of the moment. Jackson applied this intuitive, low-pre-production style in his collaborative projects with Shaw, where minimal scripting and emphasis on *"being in the moment"* defined the raw, instinctive energy of their independent films.

Later career and death

Final projects and health decline

In the late 1990s, Donald G. Jackson's filmmaking activity became increasingly limited as he focused primarily on collaborations with Scott Shaw under the *Zen Filmmaking* philosophy. His health was impacted by leukemia diagnosed in 1995, though he continued limited work and outlived initial medical expectations. By the early 2000s, his declining health resulted in reduced output, with no major directorial credits after 1998's *Armageddon Boulevard.* Jackson continued to advocate for *Zen Filmmaking* principles during this period, though physical limitations prevented substantial new productions.

Death

Donald G. Jackson passed away on October 20, 2003, at the age of 60 at UCLA Medical Center in Westwood, Los Angeles, California. He succumbed to leukemia. In his final months, Jackson endured significant pain that led to extended hospitalization at UCLA Medical Center, where he received ongoing care until his death. The obituary expressed gratitude to the doctors, nurses, and staff at UCLA Medical Center and Bowyer Clinic for their support during this period.

Legacy

Influence on independent and low-budget cinema

Donald G. Jackson is recognized as a maverick in low-budget exploitation, science fiction, and B-movie filmmaking, particularly through his adoption of Scott Shaw's *Zen Filmmaking* philosophy in later works. This approach rejected traditional scripts, storyboards, and structured planning in favor of spontaneous, scriptless production guided by immediate inspiration. Zen Filmmaking, primarily developed by Shaw, was applied in their collaborations beginning with the 1991 film *The Roller*

Blade Seven. This method often resulted in improvised, dreamlike films with minimal pre-production, placing creative responsibility heavily on actors and yielding output that frequently appeared tangled, incomprehensible, or akin to high-school video projects in visual quality and narrative coherence. Jackson's prolific output, especially from the 1990s onward (including 25 features between 1990 and 2002), exemplified dedication to low-budget creation with little regard for commercial viability or critical reception, as he produced films primarily for personal satisfaction. His work cultivated a niche cult following within underground cinema communities. Earlier films such as *Hell Comes to Frogtown* (1988), a post-apocalyptic action film co-directed with R.J. Kizer blending Mad Max-inspired wasteland aesthetics with outrageous humor and low-budget resourcefulness, earned enduring appeal among B-movie enthusiasts as a cult classic despite modest production values and initial lack of critical success. Later titles like *the Roller Blade Seven* series embraced absurd elements, reused footage, and free-form storytelling that appealed to fans of so-bad-it's-good genre fare. His legacy remains primarily confined to specialized cult audiences rather than broader independent cinema.

Scott Shaw

Scott Shaw (born September 23, 1958) is an American independent filmmaker, actor, author, and martial artist known for developing *Zen Filmmaking*—a spontaneous, scriptless method of production that emphasizes improvisation and presence over conventional planning—and for his extensive contributions to low-budget cult cinema. Born in Hollywood, California, he grew up partly in South Los Angeles before returning to Hollywood as a teenager, initially pursuing martial arts and Eastern mysticism rather than film. He is a high-ranking practitioner of Hapkido, holding 8th Degree Black Belt in the art, with certifications from organizations including the Korea Hapkido Federation. After traveling extensively in Asia during his twenties, Shaw entered the film industry in his early thirties, transitioning from acting to multifaceted roles as a producer, director, writer, editor, cinematographer, and composer. He has amassed numerous credits, largely through his prolific independent output, applying *Zen Filmmaking* principles to feature films, documentaries, and music videos that prioritize intuition and non-linear creativity. Among his most notable works are the cult action films *The Roller Blade Seven, Samurai Vampire Bikers from Hell, Guns of El Chupacabra,* and *Max Hell Frog Warrior,* which blend surreal elements, martial arts, and low-budget spectacle. In addition to filmmaking, Shaw is a prolific author of books on Zen Buddhism, martial arts philosophy, poetry, photography, and screenwriting, alongside pursuits in music and visual arts. His multifaceted career reflects a commitment to creative freedom and interdisciplinary expression across decades of independent work.

Early life

Birth and family background

Scott Shaw was born on September 23, 1958, in Los Angeles, California. He spent his early childhood in South

Central Los Angeles before returning to Hollywood for his adolescence. Publicly available information on his family background is limited. His father served in the military during World War II and earned a black belt in jujitsu. Shaw grew up in the diverse urban environment of Los Angeles.

Education and early travels

Scott Shaw's formal education focused on the social sciences and humanities, with undergraduate studies in cultural geography.He completed graduate studies in cultural and urban geography, humanities with an emphasis on literature, and Asian studies. He has taught courses on Asian studies, along with related subjects, at institutions including California State University, Los Angeles, University of California, Los Angeles, Santa Monica College, and Los Angeles Harbor College. In his late teens, after becoming a certified instructor of hatha yoga and meditation at age eighteen, Shaw embarked on his early travels to Asia. His first destination was India, where he resided in the Himalayan town of Rishikesh, studying and teaching the physical and meditative aspects of yoga. During this period, he was initiated into Buddhist, Hindu, and Sufi sects, took on the status of a sannyasa, and studied directly under teachers including Swami Satchidananda, Bhagwan Shree Rajneesh, Pir Vilayat Inayat Khan, and Thich Thien-An. Shaw then traveled to Japan, residing in Kyoto, where he deepened his understanding of meditation and the principles of Ki. Beginning in the late 1970s, these formative journeys to Asia marked the start of his lifelong pattern of extended stays and frequent returns to the region, profoundly shaping his perspectives on Eastern thought and culture.

Martial arts career

Training and expertise

Scott Shaw is a lifelong martial artist who began his training in Hapkido at the age of six, training daily in the art. He has trained in both Hapkido and Taekwondo. He is the founder of Ki Sul Kwan Hapkido and serves as president of Hapkido Taekwondo International. His expertise in these Korean martial arts has informed his work in action-oriented film roles.

Teaching and martial arts publications

Scott Shaw has been involved in martial arts instruction since his college years, when he began teaching professionally, and he has continued to offer seminars as well as instruction at colleges and universities. He founded Ki Sul Kwan Hapkido and serves as president of Hapkido Taekwondo International. His teaching emphasizes practical self-defense applications, deflection techniques using the opponent's energy, refined throwing methods for real-world effectiveness, and the integration of Ki cultivation through breath control alongside meditation for both physical power and spiritual development. Shaw has authored several instructional books on Korean martial arts, beginning with *Hapkido: The Korean Art of Self-Defense,* published by Tuttle Publications in 1996. He followed with *The Ki Process: Korean Secrets for Cultivating Dynamic Energy* from Samuel Weiser, Inc. in 1997, focusing on energy cultivation techniques. In 1998, Simon & Schuster released *The Warrior is Silent: Martial Arts and the Spiritual Path,* which explores the intersection of martial practice and spiritual growth. His works on Taekwondo include *Taekwondo Basics* from Tuttle Publications in 2002 and *Advanced Taekwondo* from the same publisher in 2006. Additional titles are *The Tao of Self-Defense* from Samuel Weiser, Inc. in 2000 and *Chi Kung for Beginners* from Llewellyn Publications in 2004. In 1994, Unique Publications produced his four-part instructional video series on Hapkido. For over three decades, Shaw has been a contributor to major martial arts magazines, including Black Belt, Tae Kwon Do Times, Inside Karate, Inside

Taekwondo, and Karate Kung Fu Illustrated. His articles cover a wide range of topics such as Hapkido joint locks, throws, deflection principles, cane and staff techniques, Taekwondo kicks and forms applications, self-defense against street attacks, Ki and Qi Gong concepts, and Korean martial arts history and philosophy. Some of these articles have been compiled into collections like Hapkido Articles on Self-Defense.

Film and television career

Acting roles

Scott Shaw has built an extensive acting career predominantly in low-budget independent cinema, with a focus on action, martial arts, sci-fi, and exploitation genres. He has amassed over 100 acting credits, many of which place him in leading or prominent roles as tough-guy heroes, vigilantes, detectives, or warriors who leverage his martial arts expertise. These performances often appear in direct-to-video or micro-budget productions known for their cult sensibilities and unconventional narratives. Shaw's on-screen acting began in the mid-1980s with a role as Jimmy T. in the television movie *Blade in Hong Kong* (1985). He gained early exposure through guest appearances on episodic television during the late 1980s and early 1990s, including roles in series such as *MacGyver* (1991), *Knots Landing* (1991), *Who's the Boss?* (1991), and *Coach* (1991). He also secured small parts in higher-profile feature films, such as a Cyberdyne technician in *Terminator 2: Judgment Day* (1991) and a cameo as himself in The Player (1992). The bulk of Shaw's acting work emerged in the 1990s and extended into subsequent decades through independent projects, where he frequently portrayed action-oriented protagonists. Representative roles include Hawk in *The Roller Blade Seven* (1991) and its sequels, Ace in *The Divine Enforcer* (1991), Alexander Hell in *Samurai Vampire Bikers from Hell* (1992), Max Hell in *Toad Warrior* (1996),

Detective Jake Blade in *Hollywood Cops* (1997) and related films, and Jack B. Quick in *Armageddon Boulevard* (1998) and *Guns of El Chupacabra* (1998). Many of these credits stem from collaborations with Donald G. Jackson, though Shaw has also appeared in standalone independent efforts featuring similar martial arts-infused, genre-driven characters. His later acting roles continued in this vein, including parts in films such as *Undercover X* (2001) as Truck Baker and *Samurai Johnny Frankenstein* (2014) as Sam Rockmore.

Directing, producing, and screenwriting

Scott Shaw has been a prolific independent filmmaker, frequently serving as director, producer, and screenwriter on his own projects, which are characterized by ultra-low-budget or no-budget production values. He holds 188 directing credits, 206 producing credits, and 75 writing credits, with most of these being self-produced micro-budget films and shorts that emphasize spontaneous creation in line with his *Zen Filmmaking* approach. Many of his works see him handling multiple roles simultaneously, reflecting a DIY ethos common to his independent output. During the 1990s and early 2000s, Shaw directed, produced, and often wrote genre-oriented feature films that blend martial arts, action, horror, and exploitation elements. Notable examples include *Max Hell Frog Warrior* (2002), where he served as director, producer (under the alias Jake Blade), and writer; *The Rock 'n Roll Cops* (2003), in similar multi-hyphenate capacities; *Vampire Boulevard* (2004); and *Vampire Sunrise* (2014). These projects exemplify his low-budget style, relying on minimal resources and improvisational techniques to create cult-oriented content. In more recent years, Shaw has maintained a high volume of output, directing numerous short and experimental films, many with location-specific themes in Japan and Berlin. Examples include titles such as *Vampire Noir* (2007), *The White Cat*

(2011), *Samurai Johnny Frankenstein Black and White* (2014), and more recent or upcoming shorts like *Kyoto in a Heartbeat* (2025), T*okyo in a Heartbeat* (2025), and *Night Falls in Shinjuku* (2025), where he continues to direct, produce, and write in his characteristic independent mode. This body of work underscores his ongoing commitment to spontaneous, resource-limited filmmaking across various formats.

Collaboration with Donald G. Jackson

Scott Shaw's collaboration with independent filmmaker Donald G. Jackson began in the early 1990s following a chance encounter when Jackson reached out to Shaw after receiving his unsolicited headshot and the two met at Gower Gulch in Hollywood. This partnership marked the birth of *Zen Filmmaking,* a spontaneous, scriptless approach to production emphasizing instantaneous creativity and spiritual intuition, with Jackson providing low-budget expertise and Shaw contributing the term and philosophical framework. Their first major joint project was *The Roller Blade Seven* (1991), directed by Jackson and co-written by Jackson and Shaw, with both serving as producers; Shaw starred as the lead character Hawk Goodman, handled editing, and composed the music. Shot on 16mm film with a modest budget, the production utilized striking locations such as the Los Angeles Dam and Griffith Observatory, incorporating innovative techniques like the *"Roller-cam"* for dynamic action sequences. The film and its immediate follow-up, *Return of the Roller Blade Seven* (completed in early 1992 and premiered at the American Film Market that year), were shot back-to-back and viewed by the filmmakers as a cohesive artistic statement in their emerging Zen style. An unauthorized re-edit by an executive producer combined footage from both into *Legend of the Roller Blade Seven,* a version neither Jackson nor Shaw endorsed due to altered editing, added narration, and removed credits, though

Shaw later released an authorized DVD edition aligning closely with the original vision. The duo continued their collaboration on additional Zen films, including *Guns of El Chupacabra* (1997), which Jackson regarded as one of their two masterpieces alongside *the Roller Blade Seven* series, inspired by a spontaneous idea from an internet article about the mythical creature. Other joint works included *Armageddon Boulevard* and *Max Hell Frog Warrior* (a re-edited version of earlier material), further exemplifying their shared commitment to unscripted, spiritually oriented independent cinema. Their partnership significantly influenced the independent film scene by pioneering low-budget, experimental filmmaking that gained cult status for its abstract style and rejection of conventional narrative structures. Jackson's death in 2003 ended their active collaboration, after which he entrusted Shaw with all rights to his films and footage to preserve their joint legacy.

Zen Filmmaking

Philosophy and principles

Zen Filmmaking is a filmmaking philosophy developed by Scott Shaw that emphasizes cinematic spontaneity, creative freedom, and mindfulness in the present moment, drawing direct inspiration from Zen Buddhist concepts of enlightenment arising naturally when one moves beyond the planning and controlling mind. The approach views filmmaking as a meditative practice where the filmmaker releases rigid preconceptions to allow the film to reveal itself organically, achieving what Shaw terms *"cinematic enlightenment."* The philosophy originated from Shaw's personal experiences in independent filmmaking, particularly in the early 1990s when abandoning a pre-written screenplay during production opened the way for more liberated and intuitive creation. At its foundation lies the complete rejection of a traditional screenplay, which

Shaw describes as a limiting device that imposes artificial structure, stifles spontaneous inspiration, and generates unrealistic expectations—especially in low-budget or independent contexts. By removing the script, *Zen Filmmaking* enables the filmmaker to respond directly to the moment, incorporating unforeseen elements and allowing the narrative to emerge naturally rather than being forced into a predetermined form. Shaw articulates several core tenets that guide the practice: making all unexpected situations work to the production's advantage; avoiding wasted resources on constructed sets by using real locations whose natural aesthetics enhance the film; acting decisively in the moment with confidence that most choices will succeed; preventing the storyline from overpowering broader artistic vision; embracing spontaneity to avoid over-planning that blocks instantaneous creative insights; and ultimately desiring nothing from the outcome so that whatever arises is inherently perfect. These principles underscore that *Zen Filmmaking* is not chaotic or unplanned randomness but a disciplined process requiring strong mental focus and clarity to sustain coherence without scripted dialogue, scenes, or structures. This philosophy contrasts sharply with traditional Hollywood filmmaking, which relies on detailed scripts, storyboards, rigid scheduling, and extensive pre-production planning that can constrain natural creativity and impose artificial limitations on the creative process. Shaw has set forth these ideas in his writings, including the book *Zen Filmmaking,* which serves as a comprehensive guide to the method, and *Zen Filmmaking: The Manifesto,* a concise declaration of its core vision prioritizing present-moment awareness and intuitive guidance over conventional constraints.

Application in his projects

Scott Shaw has applied *Zen Filmmaking* principles across multiple projects, emphasizing spontaneity, the absence of a traditional screenplay, and adaptability to whatever unfolds during production. The approach originated during the making of *The Roller Blade Seven* (1991), a collaboration with Donald G. Jackson. After an initial weekend of shooting proved disappointing due to cast performances, Shaw and Jackson abandoned the pre-written script and proceeded to film the movie while inventing the story in the moment. This decision marked the birth of *Zen Filmmaking* as a deliberate method for low- or no-budget productions, where removing rigid planning eliminates potential sources of disappointment and allows the film to emerge naturally. The same spontaneous technique carried over to the sequel Return of *the Roller Blade Seven* and to *Samurai Vampire Bikers From Hell,* which Shaw directed independently shortly afterward. These early projects exemplified tenets such as making unpredicted situations work to advantage and using real-world locations without constructed sets, relying on small crews to capture authentic aesthetics. Shaw has noted that this method requires a focused mental state akin to meditation, enabling coherent storytelling despite the lack of scripted dialogue or predefined scenes. Shaw continued applying *Zen Filmmaking* in later works, including collaborations with Jackson after their reconnection in 1996. One example is *9mm Sunrise,* originally filmed in 1996 as *Shotgun Blvd.,* with additional scenes shot in 1998 and a final re-edit in 2007 that incorporated never-before-seen material to enhance the storyline. This flexibility in editing and adding footage years later reflects the philosophy's embrace of ongoing inspiration and openness to change rather than fixed outcomes. More recent solo projects also demonstrate the approach. *The Hard Edge of Hollywood* (2008) was created as a Zen Film thriller exploring the darker aspects of low-budget filmmaking through melodrama and docudrama elements, drawing directly from real industry experiences while maintaining the spontaneous, no-script process.

Across these works, Shaw's application of *Zen Filmmaking* has consistently prioritized creative freedom and presence in the moment, resulting in films that adapt to available resources and circumstances without predetermined constraints.

Literary career

Books on spirituality, martial arts, and philosophy

Scott Shaw has authored numerous books on spirituality, martial arts, and philosophy, with a focus on integrating Eastern contemplative traditions such as Zen Buddhism and Taoism with physical practices and inner development. His works span instructional guides on martial arts techniques and energy cultivation to meditative and philosophical reflections, often emphasizing the unity of body, mind, and spirit. Many titles have been published by established presses including Inner Traditions and Weiser Books, while later works frequently appear as published editions in print and digital formats. A prominent example is *The Warrior Is Silent: Martial Arts and the Spiritual Path* (1998), which explores the spiritual foundations of Eastern martial arts practice and their essential connection to achieving mastery, presenting illustrated self-defense techniques that harness ki energy to foster balance between physical skill and spiritual growth. *Samurai Zen* (1999) provides a practical and illustrated approach to combining Zen awareness with the samurai tradition, particularly through Iaido, offering exercises for refining the senses, centering the mind and body, and cultivating higher consciousness as a path to freedom and presence. *The Tao of Self-Defense* (2001) applies Taoist principles to martial arts and self-defense, framing physical techniques within a philosophical context of harmony and natural flow. Shaw has also produced several works centered on Zen meditation and mindfulness, including *Nirvana in a Nutshell: 157 Zen Meditations,* a collection of concise meditative insights, and

Zen O'Clock: Time to Be, which encourages living in the present moment through Zen perspectives. His *"Further Zen Ramblings from the Internet"* series comprises multiple volumes of philosophical essays on Zen, consciousness, metaphysics, and existence, often presented as contemplative reflections drawn from online writings. Other notable titles address energy practices, such as *The Ki Process: Korean Secrets for Cultivating Dynamic Energy,* which details methods for developing internal energy, and introductory texts on chi kung and yoga breathing. These publications collectively highlight Shaw's emphasis on accessible spiritual and philosophical exploration through both martial and meditative lenses.

Journalism and articles

Scott Shaw has contributed extensively to journalism and periodicals, particularly in the fields of martial arts, spirituality, and film. He has been a regular contributor to major national martial arts magazines and has published numerous articles in respected industry journals. His martial arts writings have appeared in publications such as Black Belt, Tae Kwon Do Times, Inside Kung-Fu, and Martial Arts Illustrated. More than three hundred of his articles on the martial arts have been published, establishing him as a mainstay in these outlets since the late 1980s. Shaw has also written hundreds of articles on Zen Buddhism, Asian studies, and filmmaking topics. Many of these, especially on *Zen Filmmaking* philosophy and application, appear on his dedicated websites and blog, where he shares ongoing writings on spirituality, cinema, and related subjects. These shorter-form pieces often echo themes from his broader literary work on spirituality, martial arts, and philosophy.

Photography and other creative work

Photographic projects

Scott Shaw has been an avid photographer since childhood, capturing images that reflect his extensive travels and interest in spiritual and cultural landscapes. His photographic projects center on published books that document locations around the world, often emphasizing urban environments, sacred sites, and experimental visual approaches. Many of these books follow a recurring format titled *"[Location]: A Photographic Exploration,"* featuring destinations such as Bangkok, Kathmandu, Varanasi and Bodh Gaya, Tokyo, Sedona, and various cities in India, Thailand, and beyond. Several volumes highlight spiritual and Buddhist themes, including titles like *Varanasi and Bodh Gaya: Shade of the Bodhi Tree, Sedona Realm of the Vortex*, and *Snapshot Tibet.* Other works adopt stylized techniques, such as the *"Screenshot"* series depicting cities like Hong Kong and Istanbul, or variations like *Hong Kong Out of Focus* and *South Korea in a Blur.* Shaw maintains an ongoing personal photo log called The Scott Shaw Pholog, consisting of spontaneous, unposed, and unaltered images from daily life and travels, embodying his philosophy of positivity and natural observation. His photography is accessible through various online galleries and platforms, including dedicated albums on Flickr, a snapshot gallery on Tumblr, and profiles on Saatchi Art and Fine Art America. Shaw also shares recent and archival photographs on Instagram under the handle @zenfilmmaking.

Online presence and digital media

Scott Shaw maintains an official website at scottshaw.com, which serves as the central online hub for his extensive body of work and serves as a primary source for biographical details and creative output. The site encompasses sections dedicated to his books, films, music, art, biography, FAQ, Zen philosophy, Hapkido, filmmaking techniques, news, press coverage, external links, and a blog, providing a comprehensive digital archive of his contributions across multiple disciplines. A key component of his online presence is The Scott Shaw Blog, which he began composing on scottshaw.com over a decade ago and has continued as a frequent outlet for reflective prose on spirituality, philosophy, and personal responsibility. Content from the blog has been compiled into multiple published volumes known as Scott Shaw Blog Books, demonstrating the site's role in facilitating direct self-publishing and long-form dissemination of his ideas without intermediary publishers. The blog remains active, with ongoing posts that extend his philosophical teachings and Zen-oriented perspectives to a global audience through accessible digital means. Beyond the main website, Shaw extends his digital media presence through linked platforms that support his creative promotion, including a YouTube channel under *Scott Shaw Zen Filmmaking* for video content, a Dailymotion account for similar uploads, and art-focused sites such as Saatchi Art, Fine Art America, Tumblr's Scott Shaw Snapshot Gallery, Flickr's Scott Shaw Pholog, and Instagram under @zenfilmmaking. These channels collectively enable independent distribution and self-promotion of his writings, visual media, and philosophical insights, emphasizing direct engagement with audiences in alignment with his independent creative ethos. The overall online presence reflects a consistent, self-managed approach to sharing his multifaceted career and truth-seeking objectives through evolving digital formats.

Personal life and philosophy
Spiritual beliefs and lifestyle

Scott Shaw's spiritual beliefs are primarily rooted in Zen Buddhism, which he characterizes as an abstract and ultimately indefinable concept lacking any fixed essence or universal definition. He asserts that attempts to conceptualize Zen transform it into *"a something"* when its true nature is *"a nothing,"* and genuine understanding emerges only when practitioners recognize both Zen and themselves as undefined and empty of fixed form. A core principle in his philosophy is approaching every aspect of life as a new experience, unburdened by prior knowledge, expectations, worries, or emotional attachments to past events and relationships. This mindset cultivates freedom from mental constraints and promotes spontaneity, allowing individuals to engage each moment freshly and without preconception. Shaw emphasizes non-attachment to personal identity, history, and self-definition imposed by others, advocating the erasure of fixed self-narratives to foster inner wholeness and authentic presence. His writings reject spiritual materialism, guru dependency, ego-driven claims to enlightenment, and performative spirituality, instead prioritizing humble, ego-free service and conscious, intentional interaction with the world. In terms of lifestyle, Shaw promotes everyday mindfulness through positivity and small, deliberate actions, encouraging people to make the world better *"one positive word, one positive action at a time."* His personal practices draw from Zen meditation forms like zazen, breath awareness, and various yoga disciplines including hatha, raja, kundalini, and tantra, presented as practical, non-institutional tools for heightened awareness and self-control rather than rigid routines. These beliefs shape his approach to life choices, favoring presence, non-judgmental engagement, and positive intention in daily interactions while avoiding over-seriousness or attachment to outcomes. His spiritual outlook informs his broader creative work as an extension of these principles.

Current activities and legacy

Scott Shaw remains active in independent filmmaking as of the mid-2020s, producing and directing a high volume of short-form projects that adhere to his *Zen*

Filmmaking methodology, which emphasizes spontaneous creation without scripts or preconceived storylines. His recent output includes numerous shorts from 2025 and 2026, many inspired by travel locations in Japan and Germany, such as *Tokyo in a Heartbeat, Kyoto in a Heartbeat, Die Berliner Mauer,* and *Hippie Drum Circle,* where he frequently serves as producer, director, and editor. He has continued to publish writings on creative life and cinema, including *Zen Filmmaking 3: Expanded Writings on Creative Life and the Cinematic Arts,* released on November 22, 2019, which expands on his philosophical approach to independent production. Shaw sustains his engagement with photography and documentation, frequently traveling to Asia and the Middle East to capture cultural subjects in words and images shared across online platforms. He also maintains his blog and oversees related websites dedicated to his *Zen Filmmaking* principles and DVD distribution. Shaw's legacy centers on his development of *Zen Filmmaking* since 1991, a method that integrates Zen concepts of presence and intuition into low-budget cinema, influencing independent filmmakers to prioritize spontaneous creativity over traditional structures. He is further recognized for his longstanding contributions to martial arts and spiritual literature, including his status as a high-ranking practitioner and author whose works on Zen, Hapkido, and related disciplines have circulated widely in those fields.

TIME FLYS...
05/Feb/2026 02:31 PM

For those of you that have been around for a while, reading the little ditties that I place up on this page, you will/may remember that way back in the way back when I used to let you periodically know what music I was listening to on whatever specific day it used to be. *"On the Decks,"* I titled it.

I don't really do that anymore. Though, every now and then, someone will ask me, *"Why not?"* No real reason. It's just that generally I'm hearing music from all/so-many sources. Combine that with all the stuff I'm doing and I no longer, all that often, sit back and listen to an entire album.

Today, however, I had the idea to grab this one CD and pop it into my car's CD player as I drove around doing what I did this AM. The album was the only studio release by, The Wreckers.

I hadn't listened to it in quite a while. But, it's music that really stays in your mind. As I listened to it, I was reminded just how good the songs and the production were on that collection. Good stuff!

I pulled up to a stop light and got to wondering, *"Just how long ago did that album come out?"* I remember buying it very well. Back over at the Tower Records that used to be located here in the South Bay of L.A.

So, I asked Google. *"2006,"* was the answer. Wow, twenty years ago. That's crazy! It was hard to believe that so much time has/had passed. That's the same year that Tower Records shut down, at least here in the States. Still going strong in Tokyo.

I guess that's the thing about life, the longer you live, the more things are measured in your rear view. ...What was then, compared to the now. Time passes. People get old. The singers on that album are not the young women they were at the time. That's not bad or good, that's just reality.

So, here we are. We are each living what we are living. We are each experiencing what we are experiencing. We are each developing memories that brings us back to a time gone past. If you are old enough to answer this question, *"What music were you listening to twenty years ago?"* What has changed in your life? Do you still listen to those songs?

I don't know??? Maybe, like I did, you should take a stroll down Memory Lane and play that album that you used to like, from that time gone past. You never know what it may create in you or cause you to create.

* * *

05/Feb/2026 08:03 AM

Are you emerging into a better state?

A better state of mind?

A better state of being?

A better state of health?

A better state of financial wellbeing?

A better state of creativity?

A better sate of giving?

A better state of caring about and for others?

*   *   *

03/Feb/2026 12:41 PM

Just because you deny you did something does not mean that you didn’t do it.

SPAGHETTI IN TOKYO

03/Feb/2026 07:01 AM

There's this restaurant that I like to go to when I'm in Tokyo. Well… Actually, there's a few. But, for the sake of this discussion, let me tell you about this one place.

It's a small upstairs establishment. It's one of those places that if you didn't know it was there, you'd never know it was there.

It's run by two people. There's the main man, an older, some would say, elderly guy. He's the owner and the main chef. And, this very nice woman. She may be his wife. I don't know?

To get there, you go up these stairs. You tell the lady you're there. Then, she will tell you wait outside. Wait in the stairwell. Wait, even if there are available tables. Wait, until she's ready to deal with you.

When she is ready to deal with you, she will call you inside. Sit you down. Give you a menu. Then, let some time pass, and she will come back.

The thing about this establishment is, though they offer a limited menu of a few different items, the spaghetti they make there is so good! I mean, it is really-really good! Probably the best spaghetti I've ever had. Forget Italy, this is Tokyo.

If you go there, you've got to order it.

The way it works is, the lady part of the equation makes each bowl of spaghetti individually. No pre-cooked spaghetti here. So, if you're sitting there with someone, like I'm usually there with my lady, one person will get their bowl of spaghetti before the other. Don't let it get cold while waiting for the other bowl to arrive. You've got to eat it when it's warm.

I don't really know what she does or how she does it. Though you can watch her making it, as the kitchen is just behind a counter. But again, it's really-really good.

The thing is, you can tell that she makes each bowl with a one-pointed perfection, guided at excellence. No bowl is less than another. No customer is better than another. Each bowl must be done exactly as to their method.

With this as a basis, the question here is, how much of your life do you live with that level of dedicated perfection? How much one-pointed focus do you put into what you do? If you do things on that scale, great! If you don't, why not?

The truth of life is very simple. If you care enough to make each bowl of spaghetti perfect, then each bowl of spaghetti comes out perfect. If not, then it's just hit or miss. And, the main thing is, living your life on this level of perfection is a choice. What choice(s) do you make?

You can be great. You can do what you do with a focused perfection, making all that you do great. Or, you can walk the path that most people choose. Your life, your choice.

Think about it.

*　　*　　*

02/Feb/2026 02:32 PM

Owning a book that you have not read does not make you smarter.

Owning a book that you have read but will never read again does not make you more whole.

THERE IS NO CREATIVITY IN CRITICISM

02/Feb/2026 08:52 AM

For those of you with an open mind, I suppose I could end this discourse with simply the title of this piece, *"There is no creative in criticism,"* and you would immediately understand all I have to say on the subject. Of course, there's those of you out there with an argumentative mind. To each their own… So, let me say a little bit more.

I don't know about you, but I truly love vintage films. Movies from the 1940s, particularly movies that are defined by the Film Noir label, are some of my favorites. But, not just there and then, all movies created in the early years of cinematic art, I just find very interesting to watch. Just the everything about them catches my eye and my mind.

One of the main things that I find interesting about that era of filmmaking is that many of them are (supposedly) filmed in exotic locations across the globe. But, the facts be told, the majority of them were filmed right here in Hollywood and/or on studio lots in the outlying areas. No, they were not filmed in that far away somewhere. But, right here in the States.

Did anyone criticize this fact back then? Nope. That was just the way it was. No one screamed, *"That's not Paris, that's not Macau, that's not India, that's not..."*

As time in the filmmaking game evolved, location shooting (obviously) became more and more prominent. And, that certainly isn't a bad thing. But, you know, truly great films like say, *Apocalypse Now* and *Platoon* were not shot in Vietnam. They were filmed in the Philippines. If you look at the background actors, they were not Vietnamese, they were Filipino. How much heat did those films take for that fact? Very little, if any.

This is just an example of how the critical public has arisen in recent times. Then, people viewed cinema for the art. Love a film or hate a film, that was a personal choice.

But, to the essence of a production there was provided a certain acceptance, a certain, *"Suspension of belief,"* as it is titled in the industry. Now, this all seems to have changed.

I have forever had a problem with people criticizing simply because they can. In the age where we find ourselves, it seems like, as the old saying goes, *"Everyone is a critic."* Once upon a time, a person had to rise through the ranks to be found worthy of being titled, *"A critic."* They had to be good and experienced enough to actually find a publisher, and be published by someone who held the keys to an established publication. They had to have studied, perhaps earned a degree in journalism, and then move forward with their craft, based in a taught and developed understanding of the craft. Now, the gloves are off.

I think particularly as the Video Revolution came upon us, and everyone/anyone could become a Filmmaker, this also gave rise to the fact that anyone could become a Critic. But, with this/within this, something is truly lost. What is lost? There is no art in the criticism. There's only venom.

As the craft of cinema has evolved, location shooting, even at the low and no-budget level has become much more prevalent. And, that's a good thing, don't you think? Yet, where once upon a time there was no location shooting, only the pretending to be someplace the cast and crew were not, now, actually being on location has provided a source for criticism. Even in my own Zen Films, I have heard people make disparagements remarks about the places I have shot across the globe. Shouldn't that be a reason for appreciation, illuminating other cultures, not criticism? Instead, the doing, the creating, the being, and the caring enough to actually take the time to create cinematic art, all that is overlooked. All that is forgotten. But, isn't that the essence of the evolution of all forms of art in general? Isn't the doing, the doing? For it is only in the doing, that new art and new forms of art are allowed to be created.

I think it's really great that this new era has come upon us where it is so much easier to create cinematic and other forms of art. The main thing to keep in mind, however, is the fact that there are those who care enough to do, to actually create art, but then there are those who don't do that at all, and only spend their time criticizing the art others have created.

What life and lifestyle do you believe is better?

There is no creative in criticism.

* * *

31/Jan/2026 08:01 AM

There will always be a price to pay for every lie you tell.

There will always be a price to pay for everyone you hurt.

There will always be a price to pay for everything you steal.

There will always be a price to pay for everyone you judge.

There will always be a price to pay for everyone you help.

PLAYING THE GAME OF PROTEST

30/Jan/2026 01:02 PM

Certainly, at this point in history, not only is the United States but the greater world as a whole in a state of conflict. The varying sides are on polar opposites of the equation, and one believes one thing while the other believes the other. But, who is believing what and why?

When I was a child and onto coming of age, the United States was then, as well, at a time of strong opposition. Mostly, motivated by Civil Rights and the Vietnam War, people were protesting in the streets and, in fact, in some cases, getting killed by the powers-that-be.

Of course, those issues came at a time when there was a cultural revolution taking place. More and more people were believing in the fact that open expression, freedom, and enlightenment was possible. Of course, times changed but that's a different story.

At least back then, many of the people protesting had a strong reason. The draft here in the U.S. was in full effect. And, at the age of eighteen, if you couldn't present a strong reason for not joining up, you were sucked into the fray of the military and quite possibly sent to the fight in Vietnam. Many people died. I had a close family member die in Vietnam. Many came back maimed and damaged.

There was, of course, the Civil Rights Movement where people of Color were fighting for the rights they should have already been provided. Thus, many of the people protesting at that point in history had a very self-involved reason for their dissent.

Sometimes when I am driving home, I pass by the local high school. Today, as I did, I witnessed a massive crowd of young students out in front, walking back and forth across the street, carrying signs, and chanting, all during their lunch break. They were even flanked by a school security guard and, (I guess), a teacher or two controlling their moments.

I live in an affluent neighbor. Yet, there they were, all these kids of doctors and lawyer and film-producer, products of old and new money, but none of them suffering in the least, at least not financially. They were all there protesting ICE.

Now, I get it, ICE and the detention and deportation of illegal immigrates is a hot topic issue right now. The one thing to keep in mind is, the people, (at least for the most part), that are being detained are here in the U.S. illegally. The key word is, *"Illegal."*

I'm not here to debate you on this issue. I'm just stating a fact. My grandparents were immigrants who came from Scotland. But, they came here via legal channels. My lady and her family came here from South Korea via legal channels. So, I'm all for immigration, as long as it is done legally and in accordance with the law.

But, back to the point… Here were all these White kids, with a few Asians sprinkled in—like a thousand of them protesting against ICE. But, they have no skin in the game. Being from this neighborhood, they probably don't even know anyone who is worried about being deported unless they are their maid or their gardener. They just want to play the game of protest. They want that rush of adrenaline. They want to belong. Be a part of something. Feel they are guiding the world in the direction that they believe they want it to be directed. But, do they even understand what they are proclaiming or why? Do they understand the truth of the underlying issue(s)?

This whole subject has become a sore issue. And, I get it. A lot of hardcore stuff is going on.

The thing is, this is the kind of stuff that Trump proclaimed he was going to do if he returned to the presidency. He was voted into power by the masses. Love or hate his proclamations, isn't he the elected president?

Elected by The People?

The fact is, I knew when he returned he was going to reshape the sphere of the world. It's kind of like that song by Lisa, (of Black Pink Fame), *"Fuck up the world."* I knew he was going to do that. In fact, he has done less than I expected he would do.

So, love or hate what's going on, that's your choice. But, if you're a rich White kid living in a McMansion, driving a BMW to high school, and too young to vote, I don't know, do you really even understand what's going on in the world or why? Do you actually care?

Whenever I see one of these protests taking place, all it makes me think of is the Vanilla Ice song, *"Ice, Ice Baby."*

*   *   *

30/Jan/2026 09:05 AM

Think of everything that you think you know.

Think of everything that you know you know.

Think of everything that you once believed that you knew but it turned out to be false.

What does what you know matter to anyone but you?

LOOKIN' AT THE CLOUDS

26/Jan/2026 07:52 AM

How much time do you spend looking at the clouds?

In the mornings, I generally walk my lady out to her car. It's just something that I do. I tuck her in, wish her the best, close her car door, and then she is off to the nine-to-five. Me, I go back inside and dive into whatever forms of creativity I'm working on.

This morning, as I was walking back inside, I looked up to the sky, and the clouds were simply transfixing. I stood there studying them. Just pure artistic beauty.

I wasn't trying to make shapes out of them or anything like that. That thing that we have all, always, been told to do. Just viewing their etching, their essence across the sky was enough.

When I look at the clouds, this one time in my Life Time always seems to come to mind. I was in Burma back when I was about twenty-five. Pagan, to be exact. I was sitting against a tree, and the clouds had me transfixed. I remember this chai wallah, who had a nearby stand, came over and invited me to have some tea. *"For free,"* he exclaimed, when I said, *"No thanks."* The people of Burma were always so nice. He asked, *"What was I doing."* *"Looking at the clouds."* In some strange way it was like he immediately understood, he had a deep understanding of the essence of what it was I was feeling. *"Then, I will leave you to it,"* he said with a smile.

As I was looking at the clouds this morning, I realized, though they do aways seem to catch my eye, rarely, of late, do I take the time to allow their essence to totally overtake me. …Allow myself to dive into them and allow them to become a complete and total meditation.

You know, we all can allow ourselves to get caught up in the on-going-ness of life. It's really easy to get sucked into the Doing or the whatever. But, if don't take the time for silence, to truly immerse ourselves in the beauty of nature, allowing it to take hold and become a part of us, then your life, our life, my life will just pass by, and we will never have taken the time to truly embrace the pure essence of our reality.

Be careful. Don't let that happen.

How much time do you spend looking at the clouds?

WHY DO ANY HOMEWORK?

24/Jan/2026 04:39 PM

Again, I was pointed to another discussion created around the films of Donald G. Jackson and, (at least in this latest piece), to a lesser degree about myself on YouTube. When I hear these and/or when I see these presentations, it just always dumbfounds me. Don't these people have anything better to do with their life???

But, more to the point, a point I have talked and written about so many times that I cannot even remember how many… What is seemingly forever the case in these discourses is that they are always so wrong in what they say. At best, they grab a something or other here, a something or other there, salt it up with some opinion someone has said on some discussion platform and then they go on and on and on and on, making it sound like they know what they are speaking about when they do not.

The thing that grabs me the most about all of this is that The Truth is Out There! Since the dawning of the internet, I've written so much stuff about the process Don and I used in creating our movies, plus his and my filmmaking philosophy and method in general. IT IS ALL OUT THERE PEOPLE!!! You don't even have to pay for it. It is all on my website(s) and on my various other pages. And yes, there is even MORE in the books I have written on the subject! Plus, most of the movies are up on YouTube, also for free! You just have to care enough to do your homework!

Sure, there has also been the cases when someone has read what I've written, pulled a sentence here and an idea there, turned it all around and made it sound like some sort of a negative something that it was not. But, all I can say about people who live on that level of reality is, you are not providing a service. Whenever you evoke negativity, by casting your own damaging opinions is doing nothing but conjuring an ongoing flow of all that is negative. Where does that end? What does that equal?

There have also been those that I have heard or read and they have done a good job, particularly in the age when things were actually published by established sources. But, they did their research! They did their homework! Then, at least, their discourses were semi fact-based.

The truth be told, I can never bring myself to sit and listen to these highly opinionated diatribes in their entirety. Particularly when the first words out of their mouth are wrong. So, I just bounce through them. Some of the words make my smile. Others… All I can say is, (again), why don't you do your homework! It's out there for free!!!

The guy in this latest piece on YouTube didn't seem like he was basing his ideas on any level of negativity. And, that's a good thing. But, what he was saying about Don, his motivations, his creative process, who he was as a human being, and his interaction with me, and how and why I do what I do was opinion-based at best, and mostly just wrong. What he claimed was not what happened or why!

So, as is the case with most presentations on the internet, probably more people will watch his piece than read this. I doubt that he will read this. Though he should. But, as he did not do his homework before he made his production. Nor did he read any but, (at most), the minimal amount of what is out there—most probably written by someone else who also didn't live the truth or know the facts. He didn't contact me. He just talked what he talked without doing his homework.

I don't know??? What can you do???

All I can say, and this is something I have said so many times before, and that is, as someone who came from a background in academic research, I just do not understand why people don't do a full and impartial investigation and study the true facts before they present their conclusions, as that kind of analysis would never stand up to any form of critical fact checking. So, what does this type of a presentation actually equal?

And, just a word to the wise, do not believe people's opinion pretending to be facts.

CHRISTMAS IN JANUARY

23/Jan/2026 12:52 PM

I noticed that one of my neighbors still has their Christmas tree up. Christmas tree, as we approach the end of January. Why not, I thought. It should be Christmas all year long.

Not really motivate by that, but by the time to move things along, I donated approximately two thousand of my LP record collection today and I'm set up to donate about a thousand of my CDs tomorrow.

It actually took a long while to go through them all. It pretty much kind of killed two of my days.

When I dropped them off at one of my local Goodwill's this morning, two of the staff members were in awh of the albums I was donating. *"Look at this! Look at that! I remember them. I loved this song!" "Take it,"* I said. *"Keep it for yourself." "We can't,"* she exclaimed.

After I dropped off the LPs, (the CDs to be done tomorrow), I texted by lady and told her how I had filled two of the large bins at Goodwill. *"You know, you've given away thousands of dollars,"* she texted back. *"Isn't that what giving is all about,"* was my return text.

I'm sure someone will find and love those albums, at which ever store they end up.

Did it hurt to give them aways? I don't know, that's kind of a weird question/feeling, I asked myself? The fact is/was, those were all records that I hadn't played in years and probably never will again. Isn't it better to get that kind of stuff out there in the wind? Let it be a possession and an inspiration of someone who really loves it?

Yeah, it took me years and a lot of time and massive amounts of money to collect those albums and those CDs. But, pretty much everything is now streamable. It's not like the days of my younger years where you would hear a song on the radio, (or somewhere), and then you would have to search and search until you could find in on vinyl to listen to it over and over and over again. Now, even the very-very-very obscure stuff, if you know where to look, you can find it. So, it's all still available. Haveable without taking up a lot of space.

I've known a few hoarders in my life. And man, their life just becomes a mess at one point or another. Yeah, they all have a reason for collecting whatever it is they collect. But, at the end of the day, if you ain't usein' it, you ain't usein'. It means nothing to no one. It just takes up space, and I just can't believe that is a good and right and pure thing to do. Stop lying to yourself and clean up! Get the stuff out there to someone who can appreciate it!

Anyway, that's my life story for the day. And, that's my advice to all you hoarders/collectors out there. Free yourself. Give it to someone who can/will actually use it. Make it Christmas to someone every day.

MEDIUM

23/Jan/2026 07:27 AM

I was flipping channels and I came upon this Reality TV show last night. The group had invited this Psychic Medium who claims to speak with the dead.

Here's my question, if a Medium is speaking with the dead, known to that person sitting in front of them, where do those dead souls live, where do they reside? I mean, think about it, what are they doing just roaming around out there in the nowhere waiting to be contacted by this so-called Psychic to speak with their one-time loved one? I mean come on! Isn't that completely against the belief of virtually all traditional religions like Christianity? What about heaven and hell? Plus, what if no Psychic ever contacts them? What's their point to being about there, roaming around in the abyss?

I've periodically spoken about my beliefs about so-called Psychic in this blog. And, as I watched last night, that individual played the exact same game I always discuss. They ask question very subtly to get the individual to guide them in the direction where they can effectively dish out their BS. Plus, like in the case of last night, if they have the time, and know who they will be speaking with, they do research into the person so they can make their seemingly astonishing realizations.

Like I have forever said, if you sit with a Psychic and their playing this game with you, ask them a question that they could never have the answer to. A question, that there is no way they could correctly answer. Then, watch their response and their excuses.

I get it, people want to believe—people want to hear from those people they cared about that have left this life, and all of that kind of stuff. But, I believe most people don't really think about what is actually taking place and why they are believing what they are believing when it is being dished out by a Psychic.

My only advice, chart the truth before you believe. And, just because someone else tells you that something or someone is true and valid and pure of heart don't necessarily believe them.

Plus, if a Psychic Medium was a true vehicle to the great beyond, wouldn't they do what they do for free and not charge money for it?

IN THE MIND'S EYE

20/Jan/2026 07:32 AM

Have you ever had one of those situations where you have this idea to do or create that something? In your Mind's Eye it all is so clear and perfect and you have a vision of how it will turn out. But then, you do it. You do it but it doesn't turn out the way you had envisioned? Then, what? You had the vision, you did it, but when completed it was nothing as anticipated.

That kind of a thing happened to me yesterday. I had this idea to put up a shelve. I went to Home Depot, bought the shelf and the stuff I need to make it happen. I put it up. But, once it was completed, once I saw the finished product, it was nothing like I had envisioned. Now what?

First of all, I've finally realized in life that I'm not much of a DYI guy. I'm just not that good at that kind of stuff. That doesn't mean that I don't keep trying. But…

All this being said, like I have long told my filmmaking students and filmmakers in general, you may have an idea, it may be all thought out and worked out in your mind, you may have a desired end result, but you cannot hold yourself to that highly explicit standard or nothing will ever turn out the way that you hoped. This is why so many indie productions go up and are never finished. The outcome is not the outcome desired and thus the production is shut down.

Meaning, you have to be open to the outcome, even if that outcome is not what you hoped for or envisioned. You have to allow that anything you do to hold its own Zen and be what it is.

This goes to all areas of life. Think about it, what if you simply just let things be—allow the outcome to be whatever the outcome became and saw the perfection in whatever it is that was lived and/or created. Wouldn't all of life, all of the things that you do and have done then just be allowed to be art incarnate in and of itself? Think how much happier and free and fulfilled your life would be if you simply allowed things to be what they are and be whatever it is that they become. No judgement. Just Zen.

*   *   *

19/Jan/2026 07:02 AM

Everybody wants to make someone else the bad guy for their own bad decisions.

TOKYO HILTON TEE-SHIRT

18/Jan/2026 07:12 AM

As tends to be the cases, sometime(s), when I'm lost deep in the late night and I'm not doing anything of major Importance, I pop YouTube on the big screen, sit back, and a gel into the darkness while allowing the flow or the algorithm to take me from one music video to the next.

As I was sitting there last night, this video came on and one of the musicians was wearing this tee-shirt that said, *"Tokyo Hilton." "What,"* I exclaimed to my lady. *"Why don't I have one of those?"*

"Why didn't you ever buy one," was her comeback. *"Because I never saw one,"* was my exaggerated response.

Sure, sure, this was all a bit of a joke. And, the fact of the fact be told, I never wear tee-shits. But, that doesn't mean that for reasons about to be stated, I wouldn't like to own one.

Here's the thing, I have lived more than a year of my life at the Tokyo Hilton International in Shinjuku. Particularly in the '80s, when I was in and out of Tokyo all the time—sometimes for long, extended periods of time, that is where I would stay. The staff there loved me, *"Welcome back Dr. Shaw,"* every time I reappeared. I mean, I'm not exaggeration. I have lived more than a year of my life at that hotel. But, I never saw a tee-shirt.

Now, this ditty is all about one of those things of the not-too-important to anybody but the one feeling the situations. We all have these things. I mean, I'm sure you couldn't care less about a tee-shirt from the Tokyo Hilton, as it doesn't mean anything to you. But, I'm sure there are those things that if presented to you, in whatever manner that presentation may come, you would go, *"Damn, why don't I have one of those?"*

Anyway, this is just something to think about as you pass through your life. Think about it, what matters to you and why? But, perhaps even more important, why does that something matter to you at all? Why did it mean to your life? What does it mean to your life? How does it define your life? And, at the top of this conversation, what are willing to do to get it?

I GOT THERE TOO LATE

15/Jan/2026 01:56 PM

I don't know if any of you people out there are photographers? ...Well, I guess, pretty much everyone is a photographer since we've moved into the age of the iPhone. But, more than that... A real photographer... Are you a photographer?

I don't know that there's really a difference between someone who considers themselves an actual photographer and someone who just grabs some great shot every now and then on their phone. I guess the big difference is the thought process that goes into the whole thing.

For me, I've been consciously taking photographs as far back as I can remember. I got my first decent 35mm camera when I was in junior high. Loved it. I've been taking photos ever since.

The thing is... And, this is going back in time... For those of you who are on the younger side of the picture, you may not even remember the days of film. But, back then, you bought it, you shot it, you developed it, then you had everything on a print backed up by a negative or a slide.

As a photographer, back in the film era, I shot a lot of slide film. Thus, I have tons and tons of slides stuck in those metal slide holder cases. Some I have had transferred to digital. Many, however, I have not. It's expensive! And, if you have a high-end slide scanner, which you really need if you want to get a good transfer, it takes a lot of time—one slide at a time.

In any case, I had the idea that I needed to go through some of my cases of slides that have been lying around for years upon years.

The thing is, though slides are a one-time great medium, I've encountered situations where years later I would decide to look at and/or do something with a group of slides I had shot in one country or another, and they had all turned black. The image was gone. That was so upsetting. More than likely base in a bad batch of developer or fixer or both. I remember I lost all of the slides I had shot in Singapore's Chinatown before it was completely dismantled. I was so upset.

Anyway, if you are a photographer. Or, even if you dabble in the art. Maybe you have taken a deep dive into photographing one specific individual, at a very specific period of time.

When I was going through my slides today, I came upon a situation where I had done just that. I had shoot maybe ten rolls of film, focused on the face of this one young lady who I was very close to at one of the times I was residing in Bangkok.

Maybe you know how it is, when you're young and in love and all enthralled with an individual.

But, looking at the slides, I had really done a deep portraiture of this woman. I took a lot of photographs.

The thing is, I had completely forgotten about shooting those shots. Seeing them, I remembered. But, the fact of the fact be told, I had not even thought of her for many a moon. The relationship went south soon after the day I took those pictures. But, there they are, time frozen.

I've done deep photographic explorations of people before and after that time frame, in Bangkok and elsewhere. The sad thing is, and the thought that came to mind while I was studying those slides is, the woman who meant the most to me in Bangkok, I never took a single picture of her. Wow… Hard realization.

Also, while looking at the photos of that girl and then moving onto some others that were in the batch, I realized that of all of these people, all of these young ladies that I've known and have photographed, the truth be told, in each case, I had arrived too late in their life. I got there too late. They had all already been damaged and scared and walked too far down the dark path leaving them only with LESS.

Sadly, all of the people I knew in Bangkok at that point in history are no longer with us. Drugs, AIDS, and just the forced reality of the passing hands of time. I'm the only one left remembering. I'm the only one with the photographs to prove that she, (and others), existed and that they and I lived in the same space of reality, at least for a moment.

Now, everything is digital. If it's not in the cloud, it probably soon will be. Or, at least, hidden on some external hard drive or some ancient CD or DVD collecting dust and stuck in some drawer.

Actually feel it, touch it, photographs are an interesting commodity, even though they are quickly fading fast. Something to hold. Something to look at. Something to cause you to feel or re-feel. Something to make you remember a time forgotten.

But, what do they all mean? No one in my Life Circle remembers that girl but me. For anyone else to look at those slides, it would mean nothing.

It's like sometimes when I go into a thrift shop or an antique store, I see piles of old family photos being sold. To those people, to that family, those photos really meant something. They charted their time in life. They meant something, until someone cared about them no more. Then, they get tossed in a donation bin and maybe bought by someone who will never have any idea of who those people truly were, only desiring a peek into a time gone past.

So ultimately, what do those photographs, those deep character studies, based in love, lust, art, or whatever truly equal? We're here, we're gone, and what do our feelings about your feelings mean to anyone else but ourselves?

HAVE A BLESSED DAY
14/Jan/2026 01:17 PM

I always find it interesting how the colloquialisms people use change over time.

Obviously, society changes through time. As you pass through life, over longer and longer periods of time, you really come to witness how the mindset of society changes and from this the words and the sayings that people use evolve. All you have to do to take note of this progression is to simply listen to what is being said and compare that to what used to be said.

I mean, it's really a simple thing to study. Think about the things you used to say in those very unique ways, defined by the people you found yourself associating with and the society where you existed.

I think when people are young, it's really much more common that they use, for lack of a better term, *"Trendy,"* words and sayings. Whatever may be thought of as cool and culturally unique, while breaking away from the traditions of the past, that's what young people tend to utilize as their nomenclatures. As one gets older, however, it's a common practice that trendy idioms fall away, and people seem to fall more into the pattern of using a more structured and formal basis of language.

I believe that some individuals, especially those that work in customer service style jobs, are forced to communication with a much large group of people than say the person who does not. With this, they must constantly present a cordial, welcoming, and gracious demeanor.

A few years ago, after I made my purchase of that whatever from one of those customer care individuals and our dealings were culminating, she said to me, *"Have a blessed day."*

Sure, there's all of the religious connotations that can be associated with such a statement. But, beyond all of that, think about it, that's a very nice way to send someone on their way.

Since then, I've heard that expression more and more. Up until this AM, I never used it. But, maybe that will change. This morning, as my lady was heading off to her nine-to-five, with a joking smile on my face I said to her, *"Have a blessed day."* Though it was initially a joke, I really meant it. I hope she has a great day!

This is just some food for thought. We are all influenced by the people we interact with. Our moods are set into motion by the words that are spoken to us. Be all this as it may, isn't it a great thing to wish someone something good and nice as you part company?

Have a blessed day.

THE PROJECTION OF WHO YOU ARE AND WHO YOU ARE NOT

13/Jan/2026 04:04 PM

Have you ever had someone describe you to someone else and when the translation of all of that gets back to you it is hard for you to believe that someone would designate you in that manner?

Have you ever had someone tell the story about their interactions with you and the tale that they wove was completely untrue—untrue, at least from the perspective of your own understanding of what took place and your memory of that encounter?

First of all, why do people discuss other people in the first place? I suppose there are a million reason for this, but when it comes down to what it ultimate comes down to, they want their interpretation of you and how they feel about you to be what other people feel, as well. They want the world to see you the way that they see you. If this projection is based upon a perspective of love and goodness, then, I guess, it's not too bad of a thing to take place. On the other hand, if what they are saying is based in any form of negativity, then all that comes from that depiction is further resulting negativity.

In my life, I've had a number of people describe me and detail their life interaction with me. Sometimes what they say is true. Other times, however, what they are detailing is so far from the truth, at least the truth that I lived, that it is hard for me to believe. Have you ever had that happen to you?

The thing is, there is really nothing that you can do about the all of this. What they think, what they feel, what they detail, and how they want others to feel about you is solely based upon the perspective of their own limited consciousness. It comes from the place of who they are and how they witness and interact with the world.

I've had some people say some really mean and untrue things about me. In a few cases, when I once again encountered that individual, they were nothing but nice to me. Did I confront them about what they had previously said? Did I get all up in their business about it? Nope. I just let it go. Because what would my saying anything actually prove? Would it change what they had done and who they had said that something to? No.

In places in my life like the martial arts and the film game, I've had some people say some completely distorted things about me to others, describing situations and events based on a foundation of complete falsehood. Then, sometime later, they wanted or needed something from me, and all they were was full of praise. Situations like that always amuse me. Anything like that ever happened to you?

The thing is, some people wish to project their undefined life reality and unenlightened sense of that other person definition out to the world. They want the story to be told the way they want the story to be told, be it based in truth and reality or not. This is why I always warn everybody that you should never judge anyone by the way someone else describes them. You should never immediately believe a story about any other person that is being told by that someone else. Why? Because anyone who speak out about anyone else or discuss who they believe them to be is, at best, putting their own spin onto the truth of whatever reality has taken place. It is never wholly what was lived. At best, it is simply one person's conglomeration of their interactions with that someone else, while telling the tale of that life drama in a manner that, at best, only suits themselves.

KARMA AND THE TRAIN STATION THEORY

13/Jan/2026 09:21 AM

Just yesterday, I was talking about karma and the way people never seem to blame themselves when negativity comes their direction… After I wrote that, I was driving from one place to another, as life in L.A. promises, and I drove past this one location that a long-lost girlfriend and I used to visit. BAM, it sent me into one of those moments of remembrance. You know how it goes, you don't think about somebody forever and then, out of the blue, you are reminded of them, and their thought comes to your mind.

The one thought that leads to another thing happened, and I thought back to who that girl was and who she would have become.

First of all, we were together for quite a while. I was a horrible boyfriend back then. No excuses made. I was an asshole. Eventually, I met someone new and moved on. My life changed. And, I imagine hers did as well. What became of her, I really have no idea. I'm not one of those people who seeks out people from my past. I mean, why? What was, was and what's now is what's now. You know, the Train Station Theory.

Anyway, I remember her as always one of those people that took. It's just who she was, I guess. By the end of our relationship, I had given her so much money, so much stuff, took her on trips, bought her a sports car that kept breaking down, etc., etc., etc. I remember by the time of the end of our life interactions she was living over her head in WeHo and she even asked me to buy her some furniture for her apartment, which I did. I even helped her out with rent a few times. This by the time we were not even really together by any standard of definition.

Now, don't get me wrong, I was happy to help out. But, even back then, I realized that she never considered the ME in the equation, just the SHE.

As my thought-train continued, I remember she had this one longtime friend. She married a guy who already owned house. Eventually, she divorced him, got alimony, and kept his house. Now, we all know what I think about alimony and palimony and the karmic implications of such things. Even back then, both she and I thought that what her friend had done was pretty fucked up. The guy, the X, got really screwed over. All for what? Answer: Love. Love that was no longer reciprocated. Her friend walked away with a free house and tons of money. Think about the karma in that.

But, back to the flash of memoir. I've always had this weird ability to see what people will become and what they do become even if I'm not there to watch it unfold. It's just a weird aptitude I possess to understand what the pathway they are walking will lead to. I've never been wrong.

Knowing who this girl was, I'm certain that she too eventually followed the same path as her friend. It's just who she was. I'm sure she met and maybe married some guy, got divorced, received alimony, and kept the house. Again, it's just who she was, a taker.

I mean, she always promised to pay me back. Though I honestly never expected it, those are the words she spoke. Did she give me anything? Nope.

Now, you can say whatever you want about this pattern of life. Maybe you have followed it too—taking as opposed to giving. But, what is the karma in all of that?

What I have always found is that the people who walk this pathway always find a justification for their actions. Mostly, they blame the other person. They feel they are due a recompense. But, are they? Is anyone? Two people found their way together. That was a choice. They hung out for a while. That was a choice. If they weren't kidnapped, they could have left at any time. So, if the relationship goes south, if one person becomes an asshole, and/or does something that the other person considers is wrong, why should they have to pay for the further life-living and life-development of the individual who wants out? Just leave! Own your own shit!

The other thing I find with people who walk a karma-filled pathway is that maybe they try to do something good with their life post their breakup. Okay… Good for them. But, if they do it based on a dime collected from someone else, who should get that Good Karma? And, where does the Bad Karma live?

The thing is, at a person's core, they are who they are. Sure, life, life-experiences, and destiny helps to shape all of us, but from birth forward, at our essence, we are who we are and we are going to do what we do based upon that fact. Karma be dammed.

But, should karma be damned? Should it not be thought of and thought out. Should you not care about what you are doing to the other person, no matter how much you may come to blame them, become angry with them, or dislike that other individual?

Here's the fact, taking is only taking. There is no other way to describe it. Giving is only giving. There is no other way to describe it. Who are you? A giver or a taker? In all that you have done, in all that you are doing, what karma are you creating?

THE KARMA CONNECTION

12/Jan/2026 01:27 PM

I was listening to News Radio today while I was driving. One of the tales they told was about this Reality TV Star and the troubles she was currently facing.

What I've seen of her on TV is that she was a person who was always going after others in a backhanded, seditious sort of way. She caused a lot of grief to others. Now, here she is crying out, *"Woe is me!"* She wants everyone to feel sorry for her and to come to her aid.

You know, the thing is, people never look at the causation factor(s) of the negative karma that hits them. At best, all they do is cry out and want to tell the everybody who will listen to them, *"Look what's happening to me. HELP!!!"*

I mean, think about it. Think about your own life. Think about when something negative befalls you. Who do you blame? Do you blame the something or the someone out there? Or, do you take a long hard look at yourself and see how you may have set a course of events into motion that led you to where you find yourself?

I think the answer to those questions are obvious. But, maybe you are different. I don't know???

Here are a couple of things to think about:

Most people do not care about the negative impact they are having on the life of other people unless they desire to hurt them, they only care about what they are feeling and experiencing.

Most people never look at themselves, and the negative karma they have created, as the causation factor for any negativity entering their life.

The fact is, no one truly understands karma. Though philosophers, including myself, have been detailing the various aspects of karma since the birth of this understanding, there is no absolute formal.

This being said, there is a pattern that can be traced. You do or say bad things to and/or about other people, you cause pain to the life of other people, or this Life-Space, you lie, you cheat, you steal, you hurt, and negative things will come at you. We've all witnessed it. We've all seen it. All you have to do is to look to know that this is true.

But, when something negative happens to you, how often do you blame yourself?

This is just something to keep in mind as you pass through your existence. Yeah, you can always find someone or something else to blame. But, what about when the truth be told, you are the one to blame?

Think about it.

ONE DOLLAR PER PLAY

12/Jan/2026 09:29 AM

I sometimes make jokes in this blog about the fact that I've had songs that I've created that have received literarily millions of online streams and I've received only a very small pittance for all of those plays. My films, well… Some of them have received hundreds of thousands of views and I've received nothing at all.

I remember this one person interviewed me, way back in the way back when. …Seemed nice enough. They titled their article, *"Scott Shaw: How Not to Make It in Hollywood."* I thought that was a pretty funny and very telling title. I believe you can find it on this site.

It's not like I really care about chasing all of the accolades of the music and the film industry and all of that, as I learned long ago the more fame you gain the more attacks you will find that are directed at you by people who know the least about you, what you do, and why you actually do what you do. But me, like everyone, in whatever game it is that they play, we all need to earn a living.

You always hear stories about, and believe, all the tales of the creators of that whatever and how they are making loads and loads of denaro. But, how often do you hear about the fact that is not always the case?

Back in the earlier days of the film game, if you made a movie, a distributor would pick it up and give you tons of upfront money for it. Then, via the various sales to the international marketplace places, a lot more money could be made.

Then, the Video Revolution hit, and everyone became a filmmaker. Add to this the rise of possibilities on the internet, and forget about it, if you weren't playing the game in the BIGS, the A-Market, there was little to no money to be made.

Sure, for a time there was the Video Tape market, followed by the DVD and later Blu-ray transformation where some money could be made. But then/now, that era is all but gone. I mean, ask yourself, when was the last time you watched a VHS or a DVD? It's over!

Streaming is now the name of the game. And with that, someone is making money. But, most probably, not the filmmaker.

Like all people in the Film Game, I too have followed the trends towards Streaming. But, in that trend, someone is making money but not me.

I kind of smile when I see the numbers for some of my films on YouTube. …Which are up there for FREE! But, keep in mind, because they have nudity and other such non-condoned items in them, I can't even links ads to them, to make a hundredths of a cent if someone clicks on something. I guess YouTube is making money on each view, but not me.

Like my film, *Naked Avenger,* for example, as I write this, there has been one million seven hundred thousand views. Just think, if I only got one dollar per view, which I think would be a very reasonable fee to pay, I would have over a million dollars in my bank account. How much money have I made on it since it has been up on YouTube? Zero. My film, *Shotgun Blvd.,* three-hundred and fifty-three thousand, three hundred views. Add one dollar per view to that, and… But, what have I received? Nada. Absolutely nothing.

Now, in all truth, I am happy that my films are out there, and I'm happy that some people seem to enjoy watching them. But… And, this is an important thing to keep in mind, if you are watching something for free, either on a site like YouTube or via some bootlegged unauthorized copy on some website based in some far-off foreign country with no copyright laws, the person and the people who made that film are receiving nothing. What's the karma in that for you?

So, here's what we should do, set a payment method in place where for each time you, (or anybody), has watched, (in the past, present, or future), one of my films, I get one dollar. Whenever anyone watches footages from my films, used by some Content Creator, or a detailed bashing review of one of my films, I get one dollar. Small price to pay don't you think?

I'm just joking, of course. But, in all that you do—in all that you consume, are you being fair, just, and honorable to the person who created that whatever. If you are, great! Good for you! If not, what will be your karmic price?

THE PRICE OF CHASING YOUR DREAMS

10/Jan/2026 08:12 AM

I watched the 2023 movie, *Americana,* last night on STARZ. Interesting movie, though the storyline had a few problems. But, beyond all of that, the plot follows, at least in part, Sydney Sweeney's character in a quest to get to Nashville where she could become a well-known singer. At the end of the film, she ends up with a hundred thousand dollars and is apparently making her way Nashville's direction.

Though that was just a partial plot of the film, as there were so many stories going on within one another. A cinematic technique that I love. It did send me to thinking about the chasing of a dream.

It's an old story that I've told before, but as that story goes, I grew up in Hollywood, a place where so many dream of finding fame and fortune. Even by the time I was attending Hollywood High School I knew people and knew the children of some people who were both very successful and those who were questing for that fame they knew for only a moment. As I moved into the filmmaking game, much later in my life, I encountered so many people who had come to Hollywood believing that they had what it takes to, *"Make it."* Some, like Sweeney's character, even had the financial backing behind them. What happened with their career? I have no idea. It went nowhere. This, though so many of them told me, *"They would be the one that would make it, and I would be the one who was lucky if I put them in a film."* The few who did make a name of themselves, however, were the ones with no ego, just a directed quest.

This is the thing, there is the dream and there is the reality. And, it's very hard to define if a dream can become a reality.

Yes certainly, some people do come to places like Nashville and Hollywood and their dreams do reach reality status. But, we have all heard the stories of those who have not made that jump. Most of those who hold that dream or have that belief in themselves do not make it.

But, in fact, even one of the central characters of the film, Americana, he and I used to end up at auditions together all the time. There he is in that film, and here I am, the lowly Zen Filmmaker, writing this piece of nonsense. So???

Yesterday, I went into this thrift shop. Just ahead of me, walking through the door, was this guy dressed up and looking exactly like Andrew Eldridge of Sisters of Mercy fame did back in the 80s. He wore black pants, a long black coat, a black hat, black aviator sunglasses, and had his shoulder length hair dyed black. I guess he was attempting to emulate that something of a person of a time gone past.

Now, to this day, The Sisters of Mercy are one of my all-time favorite bands. But… I never tried to dress like the lead singer of the band.

This is not an uncommon thing, people believing that if they emulate the vibe of a famous person, they too may reach that level of fame. I've encountered several people who do and have done this. But, impersonating is never a formula for success. That's just, at best, playing a Mind Game with yourself while paying tribute to that person you can never be.

The guy, the moment he walked in, asked the person at the counter, *"Do you have any keyboards?"* The answer was, *"No."* What did he think the place was, Guitar Center? He turned and left.

All this feeds into the promise and the progress of your life and your pursuit of your dream. It gives you food for thought. Particularly, in this day and age, where you no longer have to travel to places like Nashville or Hollywood to make the possibility of your dream come true. All you have to do is to actually pursue it. Do it.

But, more than all that, what is your dream and why do you hold that dream? Because the fact of the fact always is, whatever you believe that far off something to be, it will never be what you expect it to be. So, in your walking that path to whatever it is that you desire, what will be the cost to your life, the cost to the life of others, and what about your karmic destiny? Remember, once you do something it can never be undone. And, though you may lie to others about what you've done and why you've done it, you can lie to yourself about what you've done and why you've done it, but, once you've done it, it is done, then what?

SITUATIONS CREATED BY OTHERS

08/Jan/2026 07:35 AM

Have you ever had one of those life situations that was not a wanted thing, that was not a good thing, but it was created by someone else?

There is a lot of ways this can happen. But, the main component in it is the fact that you did not set the situation into motion. It was instigated by someone else.

Have you ever had that happen—that something that altered your life in a negative manner, but it was not something that you did to yourself?

I would guess that something like that has happened to most of us. I know it has happened to me. Maybe it was something small. A momentary reality that was not desired; it was here and then it was gone. Or, maybe it was something much larger. A big BANG where somebody did something to you that changed the entire progression of your life.

Why don't you take a moment right now and think about this. Truly take a look at the evolution of your life. Was there someone who did something to you that changed your pattern of progression and development in a negative manner, be it small or large?

Now, that you have that situation in your mind, what did you do about it?

In some of the cases, some people go all revenge crazy. They try to hurt back.

Has that ever happened to you? Have you ever done something to someone else that they did not like and they tried to hurt your life because of the occurrence? If they did, what did that do to your life? Did it actually hurt you back? And, after the doing of the revenge focused deed, what occurred in your life?

Have you ever tried to do that to someone else's life? They hurt you, so you wanted to hurt them. If you have followed that path, what was the result? Did it make you feel better? Did it actually hurt them? Or, did you just set an entirely new trend of negativity into life-motion where hurt only equals more hurt and the cycle continues?

The thing about life, what is hurtful to one person maybe be helpful to another. If you love hell, it becomes heaven.

On an even deeper level, it comes down to the fact about how you process the hurt unleashed by someone else because stuff like this sadly happens to everyone at one point or another in their life. You can take it as pain and feel all of the feelings associated with such a thing, or you choose to transcend the negativity of what was done to you, turn it around, and either try to learn from it or to create something positive out of the rubble. That's not easy, but it can be done. How can it be done? By changing the definition of the action that was done to you in your own mind thus redefining the outcome.

Have you ever encountered someone, who actually liked the pain—liked to suffer. There's a of them out there. I've known people that when they were hit, would say, *"Hit me again."* I've also known people who have wallowed in the suffering or negativity, in whatever form that would take. What happened to the life of these people? The answer is different for each. The point being, and these are exaggerated examples, but if you can transcend the negativity of what was done to you, not only do you beat the doer at their own game, but you overcome any negative thoughts and feelings, and thereby come to a better, more powerful state of being. From this, not only do your rise your consciousness to a higher state of understanding, and minimalize the effect of what was done to you, but you prove, without saying or doing anything, that you are more than any person who would unleash negative actions upon anyone.

THIS IS PUNK ROCK!
07/Jan/2026 08:10 AM

Kinda funny… I was having a talk with this one guy about the this and the that of various films and filmmaking in general. You know how it goes, those who are into such things discuss the variants and the subtitles of the craft. At one point he makes the statement that he noticed how in at least one of my films the audio was not all that perfect and he had to adjust the volume on his TV as he was watching it. Immediately, *"This is Punk Rock! There's no rules! Who gives a fuck about that kind of thing,"* I exclaim.

And, I think that that's the thing that so many people have misunderstood about *Zen Filmmaking* since its inception. Me, and none of us, who make Zen Films, are attempting to make films defined by what has come before.

I mean, for someone like me, who came up in the beginning of punk, it was so freeing! Me, a classically trained guitarist, who was influenced by the works of virtuosos like John McLaughlin and Al Di Meola, it was an orgasm to be able to throw all that theory and technique out the window and just play.

That's what *Zen Filmmaking* is. It's punk, it's freeform jazz, it's freedom. The stories, fuck 'em. They've all been told. It's all about the visuals, the feeling, the essence. If the sound isn't all that perfect, then that's the perfection in itself.

I guess it's just me, but I am always so surprised when people still don't get. I'm mean, I've spoken and written about *Zen Filmmaking* for more than three decades by this point in time. Yet, all anyone tries to do is compare a Zen Film to a traditional film. It's not! It's a Zen Film! It's Punk Rock!

Anyway…

NICHE SUBJECT MATTER

06/Jan/2026 09:04 AM

I don't know if this is a good or a bad thing, as it puts a timeline on my age. Well, of course, I have nothing to hide about my age—not like some people do. And, in fact, I'm very happy and surprised to have made it this far in life, as I never expected to. But, I'm getting way too far off subject here…

Anyway…

I'm one of the OG's on the internet. I was one of the early people to partake of what was to become, long before it was even called the internet. No, I wasn't using it in the 1960s when it was called, ARPANET, and basically used for the military. But, I was there when it was first opening up to the wider public.

I got on it at a time when I was in Grad School and doing research for my Ph.D. It opened up so many more options. I was able to read research papers and articles from newspaper from afar, right in my own home, which was my apartment in Hermosa Beach. It was great. This was long before personal websites, social media, and the like.

I watched it evolve. I was there as it evolved. And, I have often found its evolution curious, while also witnessing the very negative aspects of it. We all know about those.

As the evolution has moved to AI over the past couple of years, I have become very enthralled with what has taken place. The level of information that can be had, is so much more haveable. Though, through my own research, what is presented, in many cases, is very biased.

I mean, at least in the Right Now, AI only grabs from what is already out there. So, if a lot of one side of the argument is being propagated across the web, that is what AI picks up on.

I've spoken about this is the deep past, here in this blog, about search on Google, (which is obviously the main search site across the globe). But, back in the day, when someone wanted info on Hapkido for example, articles on my site would be some of the first to come up. All Good. Happy to be of service. Now, that's not the case. But, why? What changed? Even in the search of and for Scott Shaw, I have fallen by the wayside.

In some ways I find that very interesting, in that, (and I've told this story in the past), back in the day, not all that many years ago, the cartoonists Scott Shaw, (who I've never met), did not even come in the search for Scott Shaw, even though he had produced massive amounts of products. I was the one who actually contacted Google, back when you could do such things, and suggested they put him into their search. Which they did. Now, he is there and I am gone. Well not gone, but not near as prominent as I once was.

And, please know, this is not a thing about ego or anything like that, it is just a thing about life and the reality of the age in which we live.

In a moment I am going to show you what Google AI has to say to about me and this situation. But, before that, I want you to take a moment and to think about how you interact with the information that is provided to you on the internet. Of course, as the old joke goes, *"The internet never lies,"* when we all know that to not be the case.

I mean, just last weekend, I wanted to check and see if this flea market I like to go to was going to be open, as it has been raining really hard here in L.A. over the past few days. Google said, *"Yes,"* it would be open. I get up early, drive all the way over there, and nana, it was closed. While driving away, I decide to check again. This time Google said, *"No, closed."* Annoying! That's just an example about the truth of the internet.

How much information that you find on the internet do you instantly believe? I'm not even going to go into the whole deal with Content Creators and Trolls and all of the people who have nothing better to do than to spout their opinions, as wrong as their opinions may be, but just the internet, just Google for example, how much do you instantly believe? And, maybe the better question should be, how much should you believe?

Really think about this… Think about this the next time you ask a question of that Wizard of Oz, hidden behind the veil of Google.

As for Googles definition of me… Here it is, as they title it—as Google titles me, Niche Subject Matter.

Scott Shaw: Niche Subject Matter:

Niche subject matter: The Scott Shaw who is an author is primarily known for writing numerous books and articles on Eastern philosophy, Zen Buddhism, Yoga, and martial arts, particularly Hapkido. While he has published extensively with reputable publishers like Simon & Schuster and Tuttle Publishing, these topics appeal to a specific audience, which results in a less "prominent" general public visibility compared to a mainstream fiction author.

Diverse publication types: His writing career includes poetry, literary fiction in journals, and non-fiction books, which can make it harder to categorize him as a single, highly visible "author" of a breakout bestseller in general searches.

"Zen Filmmaking" focus: He is also an actor and filmmaker who created a unique, free-form "Zen Filmmaking" style, a niche pursuit that further diversifies his profile away from traditional authorship.

In essence, his online presence is a reflection of a prolific career spread across numerous specialized fields, rather than a lack of achievement. He is well-known within his specific communities (martial arts, niche philosophy, classic animation history) but not a general "author" in the popular cultural sense.

+ If you want to know about why they say my music is so often overlooked in regards to my bio, read away:

Scott Shaw: Genre and Niche Focus:

Scott Shaw's music career is often overshadowed by his high-profile work in martial arts and independent film. While he is a prolific multi-instrumentalist with a vast discography on

Apple Music, Spotify, and Tidal, several factors contribute to its rare mention:

Dominance of "Zen Filmmaking": Shaw is most widely recognized as the creator of Zen Filmmaking, a scriptless, spontaneous method of production. This unique cinematic philosophy, alongside his cult classics like The Roller Blade Seven, tends to be the primary focus of his public identity.

Music as a Functional Tool: Much of Shaw's musical output is inextricably linked to his films. He frequently creates the soundtracks for his own features and music videos, leading many to view his musicianship as a component of his filmmaking rather than a standalone career.

Martial Arts Prominence: Shaw is a highly respected teacher and author in the martial arts community, having published over 300 articles and numerous books on the subject. This extensive body of work often takes precedence in biographical discussions.

Genre and Niche Focus: His current musical focus on Trance, Electronica, and Soundscapes targets a specialized audience rather than the mainstream pop or rock circles.

Intentional Humility: Similar to other prolific creators, Shaw has expressed that for him, the "music is the point" rather than personal fame. He often prioritizes the artistic process and helping others in the industry over seeking mainstream recognition for his individual music releases.

I guess Google AI thinks my middle name should be, *"Niche."* ☺

*   *   *

05/Jan/2026 04:19 PM

If you saw all of the people that you were close to in the past but are close to no longer, what would you say to them?

THE WRITING IS ON THE WALL BUT IF YOU DON'T READ IT NOTHING IS LEARNED

04/Jan/2026 03:14 PM

What will happen next in your life is very self-evident. It is very easy to see what the path you are walking will equal in the long run. The thing is, most people never take the time to study and be honest enough with themselves to realize how, as the old saying goes, the writing is on the wall.

Most people live in a delusional illusion about how what they are doing is not only affecting their own life but the life of all those they interact with. People want to believe what they want to believe, and they want to believe that what they are doing will cause them become the person they wish to become. The problem is, there is more than a fine life between belief and reality, between dreams and actualization.

There is a certain reality experienced in all people's lives that when they are young. That reality is, the world is out there for them to grab. There is time and with that time there is still time for them to live their dreamed of existence. For some, if they walk a path that will truly lead them towards living that reality, if they learn the skillset that it will take them to achieve that reality, if they pay the price, (whatever that price may be), and do what it is they must do, then they may actually ascend to reach their dreams. The fact of the fact is, however, even if someone pushes the buttons on all of those components, the dreamed of existence is only achieved by a very few. And, the most important element in all of this is, the bigger the dream, the harder it is to achieve. Thus, many/most are left with a life lived with less.

There are some who do walk their way up the ladder. But, in this becomes one of the biggest complications of all life complications. How did they get there? How many lives did they hurt in their ascent? And, what did they do with any achievements they achieved? Did they use it to hurt, or did they use it to help?

Again, returning to the component of youth, in youth, in association with achievement, many a person views their life via the framework that whatever success they achieve will continue and it will rise up from there. But, all anyone has to do is to view the life of someone who did rise to success, but did so on the backs of others, hurting while they ascended, and via time it becomes very clear that they fall/that they eventually fail. The example(s) of this are legion. Yet, so few people ever even consider this fact. And yes, it is a fact.

What you really need to think about as you pass through your life, and as you strive to reach your desired level of success, is what are you doing, what overall, wide spanning implications does it hold, and who are you affecting as you do what you do? The path in front of you is always defined by the karma you create as you walk it—from your very small actions, to your very large ones.

Right now, take a moment, wherever you find yourself in your life, and define, what has the life path you have chosen revealed? As you walked your path, right now, forget about what you learned along the way, but truly focus on where you have ended up. In retrospect, if you simply would have watched the signs, was it not clear when you began your travels where you would ultimately have ended up? Would it not have been more clear if you simply would have honestly taken the time to study the path, study yourself as you walked the path, and studied the direction that path was leading you? Could your end result not have been easily predicted?

The fact of life is, if you have no desires, achieving them is very-very easy. For any desire you hold, however, there will be a price. Complications arises when you are not the only one paying that price, but when you involve others in your assentation.

The writing is on the wall, but are you willing to read what it has to say? Right now, where is what you are doing leading you? Be truly honest with yourself, where is what you are doing leading you and how is what you are doing affecting others?

TO BE CONTINUED

03/Jan/2026 03:57 PM

I finally got around the watching the TV Series, *Shantaram* on Apple TV. It's a pretty good series shot in India, starring Charlie Hunnam. Though it has a few problems in its story development, like I would care about such things, as per all of you movie critics out there attacking my filmmaking style and myself about such matters. ☺

Overall thought, it truly illustrates the grittiness and violence that happens in India. …Like I have long said, India is one of the most violent places on the earth. Anyway…

The series concludes with Hunnam's character being bound by rope, with his hand tied above his head. As he is hanging there, he is being beaten by a police officer by what sounds to be a chain. Very violent and a penetrating scene. The kind you just don't want to think about.

As he is hanging there, being beating, the message comes on the screen, *"To be continued."*

Obviously, they planned to do a second season of the show. But, after reading about the series, it was apparently not well received, and the series ended with that horrible image. My lady says, *"That means his beating is what is to be continued."* She was obviously being tongue in cheek. But, that was it. Pretty much the last image placed in your mind.

Now, there have been a few series I remember that have ended with a major cliff hanger. And, though they obviously planned to continue the storyline, the show got cancelled, so the audience was just left to wonder, *"What if..."*

And sure, it's just a TV show. It's not real. But, what does that say about life, reality, who control what and why? If someone has the power to first of all create something, as negative as that something may be, and then to just let it lay there, permeating though space and time having concluded, *"Not to be continued,"* with no positive outcome.

This is why I don't like horror films. This is why, so often, when I see someone being hurt or tortured or whatevered in a film or on TV, I just turn it off.

It is never good to put negativity out there, on any level. Be it real or be it fiction. Hurt and negativity only equals hurt and negativity. That's the simple truth of life.

Think about that as you do whatever it is you do—as you create whatever it is you create. Do you wish to leave people with an image of horror and hurt in their mind? Or, do you wish to leave them with an image of love, peace, happiness, kindness, and goodness?

THE MORE ANGRY YOU GET THE LESS ICE CREAM YOU GET

01/Jan/2026 04:44 PM

Kinda funny… I was in a café today that also sells gelato, and this young Korean family came in. The little girl picked out what flavor of gelato she wanted and went and sat down at the table her parents pointed her to. The couple ordered whatever it was that they wanted and then brought the gelato to the young girl in a cup.

For some, (unknown to me), reason, the little girl was not happy with something. She wasn't really throwing a fit or anything, but I guess she was being disagreeable to her parents. The father leans into her and says, *"The more angry you get the less ice cream you get."* With that, he reaches in and takes a bite from the cup. Immediately, the demeanor of the young girl changes. She takes the spoon and grabs a bit of the gelato.

I could not help but smile. How profound! *"The more angry you get the less ice cream you get."* That is so like life. The more anger you feel, the more problems you cause, the less you get to live your best life.

How about you, how much anger do you feel? How many problems for others have you caused? And, in doing so, how has that harmed the evolution of your life?

A bit later in the day, I was driving home with my lady. There is this one cliffside bay that I always like to stop at, and take a look at, when I have the time. It's very breathtaking and beautiful. The thing was/is, it has been raining very hard over the past few days in my area, and the ground was totally soaked. Meaning, thought there was tons of green grass on the ground, our shoes got completely impacted with mud.

I know this area. I knew that would happen. But, I didn't think about it. Didn't think about it, until I thought about it. Walking back to the car, I knew it was going to be a mess. I remember the last time I did it. It took forever to clean my shoes.

Me, I was wearing this new pair of tennis shoes I had just bought and really liked, and my lady wore these combat boots. I could only imagine, what a mess it would be to clean them. I was really pissed at myself.

We get home, and the clean-up begins. Me, with my shoes, and for her, her boots. What a mess!!! The mud was caked on, caked in so deep.

Though I was throwing a bit of a fit in my mind... You know how it goes when life is all going along so well, then you are hit with something you really do not want to be dealing with. But, all you can do, is do. Which is what I did.

As I was doing, I flashed back to what that young father said to his daughter, *"The more angry you get the less ice cream you get."* I smiled. I realized I had to make the whole process a meditation, not an undesired, angry-making, chore.

This is all just something to think about the nexttime that something happens to you and it really pisses you off. No matter what the cause—no matter who caused it, remember, *"The more angry you get the less ice cream you get."*

*   *   *

30/Dec/2025 01:24 PM

Who's life, besides your own, are you trying to make better right now?

* * *

30/Dec/2025 10:16 AM

You can focus on and point out the things that are right or you can focus on and point out the things that are wrong.

Your life. Your choice.

*   *   *

30/Dec/2025 10:07 AM

If a person does not pay respect to others, that means that they do not respect themselves.

WHAT YOUR MOTHER MAKES YOU

30/Dec/2025 10:01 AM

Back in the day, I'm referring to the 1960s and the 1970s, people would often say, *"That's your mother talking,"* when someone would say something based in an old or repressive way of thinking. Mostly, I found, that someone would make that statement when they did not like or did not agree with what someone was saying and they wanted them to behave in some other manner. In my mind, when I would hear that statement, sometimes, I would mentally voice, *"No that's your mother talking."*

All of this was based around the fact that during that period of history, people, and human consciousness, was seemingly rapidly evolving. Or, at least, so it seemed. And, the human race, at least those who cared to embrace such things, were walking and believed in a newly formed path to absolute freedom. Free from all of the dogma of times gone past.

Yeah, that period didn't last. Then came a time of intensified self-ish-ness and self-full-ness. That time, instigated in the 1980s, has remained the period we find ourselves in today. Especially since the dawning of the internet and the birth of Content Creator culture.

All this be as it may, yes, your mother is speaking through you. Yes, your father is speaking through you. Think about it… No really, truly think about this, how many traits do you exhibit that were first presented to you via your parents? How many behaviors do you hold that you, perhaps unknowingly, express that were used by your parents?

A lot of people wish to deny this fact. They wish to claim that they are nothing like their parents. And, perhaps it is true that they have tried to excommunicate their parents from their mind and their lifestyle as much as possible. Nonetheless, though a whole lot of denial may be taking place, there is no way that any person who is raised by an individual does not have, at least hidden somewhere down inside of themselves, ideas, actions, and traits that were taught to them by that other person.

From my own perspective, I have spent my whole life walking a different path than that which was forged by my parents. I feel like I had some pretty fucked up parents and I don't have a lot of good feelings about them due to the life and the lifestyle they caused me to live as a young person, and the things that I encountered due to their lack of awareness about their child. Just so you know where I'm coming from…

This being stated, I, every now and then, will see some thoughts, traits, physical actions that I first witnessed expressed by one of my parents. It's inevitable.

So, take a moment right now and think this through. Really, chart this out. What do you do, how do you think, what life-actions do you express, that were first brought to you by your parents? Really define a few of these. Bring them into focus.

Now that you have these ideas in place, what have they caused you to do? How have they caused you to act? What have they caused you to unleash onto the life of others? And mostly, how have they affected the overall development and evolution of your life?

By taking the time to know and understand this, it will allow you to hold a deep and penetrating mirror into your life, your lifestyle, what you have lived, what you have become, and perhaps even what you will ultimately become.

MEDITATION THAT NO ONE UNDERSTANDS

29/Dec/2025 08:04 AM

I've been thinking to write a piece about the intricacies of meditation and why so few people truly understand the subtle elements of the true essence of meditation for the past couple of day… …I've been really busy with other projects, so I haven't been blogging a lot of late. Sorry…

Anyway, I went out to breakfast this AM. My lady and I went to this restaurant that we visit not infrequently. As we walk in, I hear the song, *Do You Remember,* by Phil Collins playing over the sound system. I didn't really think too much about it. Then, maybe ten minutes into the session, I begin to realize, wait a minute, that song is in a loop. It's on replay. So, for the next forty-five minutes or so, the staff, the one other customer in the establishment, and my lady and I, we heard that song over and over and over again. I wanted to scream!

Now, for you Phil Collins fans out there, don't get me wrong, I certainly respect the man for his accomplishments and his music, but in a loop, come on, are you kidding me! I wondered if he was getting his royality payment for each time that song was played? ☺

Now, all this brings us to the point of the piece I was going to write… What is meditation? And, why do so few people truly understand the process and the practice?

When most people think about meditation, they envision someone sitting, with their legs crossed, and their eyes closed. And sure, that is an ideal example of meditation. Zazen as it is known in Zen Buddhism.

But, the vast nature of meditation is much grander than all of that. In fact, meditation can encompass so many elements of life, that there is no true hard and fast rule about what is or is not a meditation. Here. This is where the misunderstanding of meditation begins to arise. Most people only think of it as one thing. That sitting thing. But, it is much more than that.

Particularly and historically with the rise of Zen Buddhism in Japan, meditation began to vastly expand in its understand. Certainly, Kinhin or walking meditation is now a more commonly known and recognized practice. But, the practice of meditation fans out from there.

In other traditions, such as the Sufi tradition, for example, the Whirling Dervishes are an ideal example of true movement meditation. They spin. It's an incredible sight.

As you may know, I was very closely associated with the Sufi Order in my early years. And, I was luckily enough to witness the Whirling Dervishes exhibit their advanced meditative skillset in a very small and intimate setting. It was incredible!

This is the thing, I could go into all kind of examples of the various forms of meditation: known or unknown but it would all come down to one factor. That factor is, meditation is what you choose to make it. Yes, you can follow the longstanding teaching of meditation, like Zazen, Mantra Meditation, Wall Staring, and all of those. Or, you can view the more nuanced versions. But, if you do not meditate, if you do not take the time to consciously separate your mind from the chaos of life, then all you are is dominated by your desires, your whims, and the emotional exploitation shifted onto you by others.

So, here's the question… Can you quiet your mind? If you can, great! If you can't, why not? And, if you do not try, if you cannot do it, do you not understand that you are missing one of the greatest elements of your human life, the removal of all of that chaotic rumbling around causing you to lose your peace.

There are many schools of meditation that teach their practitioners to listen to a sound and be drawn into it. So, is listing to a Phil Collins song over and over and over again a meditation. If you make it so, if you choose that as your pathway, the answer is, yes. If not, it is just purgatory.

And here is the Truth Point, if you can consciously and purposefully choose your mediative path, anything can become your tool for silencing and focusing your mind. But, you must make a very conscious, very precise, and very practiced technique. You must do it all the time, or it becomes nothing more than a Mind Game.

THE GIFTS THAT YOU DON'T WANT

24/Dec/2025 07:48 AM

Kinda funny… In my feed yesterday, on IG, came a segment about kids and adolescents that didn't like the presents that they received on Christmas. It was pretty hardcore. I mean some of these young people received gifts like TVs and the like and in one case the young man threw it on the floor and stomped on it because he wanted a Samsung and not the brand that he was given. WOW! It went on from there. Funny, from someone on the outside. But, I'm sure it was not funny for the parents who took the time and spent their money in order to give their child what they thought they wanted.

I don't know about you, but I never really got the gift I wanted on Christmas either. I certainly would not have behaved like those young people did or my ass would have been kicked by my father. They were just disrespectful and unappreciative. And, I was taught to never behave in that manner. Me, I just smiled and thanked my parents and was thankful for that anything I actually did receive.

I think the ideal example of all this came when I was a young teenager. Synthesizer had hit the market a number of years before, but they were way too expensive for someone like me to afford. A few months before Christmas, when I was like fourteen, Korg released the Mini-Korg. I would go and play it at my local music store, and I really believed that it would change my life if I could get one. It's cost a very affordable, (affordable compared to Moogs and Arps of the era), $395.00. Christmas was coming around. I told my mother about it. Told her how much it was. How much I really wanted it. What it would mean to my life. Where to go and buy it. Christmas morning arrives. I was all full of anticipation and hope. What did she buy me? An autoharp. I was very-very sad. What the fuck was going to do with an autoharp? But, I thanked her. At least she cared enough to try. But, I truly believe not getting one of the Mini-Korgs, and not being able to personally afford a synthesizer for a few more years, truly altered the evolution of my life. That's why, in the case of my nephew, who by fourteen was already an accomplished musician putting out his music, I try to hook him up with whatever he wants or needs to create. I hope to give him the chance that I never had.

As adulthood came, some years I received no Christmas gifts at all. But, I guess that's just life.

On the same note, a few days back, I ordered a new Les Paul from the Gibson factory in Nashville. It's a model that's apparently exclusive only to the factory release. It got here fast. In like two days. I opened it up after UPS dropped it off yesterday afternoon. The guitar immediately disappointed me. Not a bad guitar on the grand scheme of things. But, less than what I expected. Life??? Christmas???

So, here we are. It's Christmas Eve. Christmas is tomorrow. Hanukkah has already passed. Did you get what you wanted? Do you anticipate getting what you truly want? Did you get your loved one(s) what they truly wanted? Did you get them anything? Did you get that person who you care about anything? Did you get them what they truly wanted? Did you care enough to get that person that you do not even personally know, but perhaps know of or some-time encounter, anything? Did you even bother to think about them?

Life is all based on who you care about, what you care about, and what you can afford to give to others. Sure, that's the facts. But, if you don't care enough to care enough to understand what those outside of yourself truly want or need, what does that say about you?

And here, this, this brings us to the flash point of desire. As The Buddha said, *"The cause of suffering is desire."*

Desire… This is something that few people even consider. They do not consider what they desire or what their desire(s) are doing to their life or to the life of others. They simply Want. But, in that wanting what is created?

For some, what they, *"Want,"* what they desired, is focused upon a higher goal. For most, however, like those in that piece on the Gram, they just want what they want and when they don't get it, they throw a fit.

How about you? Where do you fit into this equation? Where do you fit into the game of, *"What you want?"*

One of the greatest and/or most important things I find about the Spiritual Path is, it really schools one into watching their desires, understanding their desires, taking hold of their desires, and ultimately controlling their desires. For if you live a life bound by desire, if you live a life controlled by desire, you will forever be unfulfilled.

So, think about it… What have your desires meant to your life? What have your desires done to your life? What have you done to accomplish your desires? Did you harm anyone in the process of your gaining your desires? If you did, what does that mean to your karma? What does that mean to your ultimate life definition?

Also, what have the desires of others done to your life? What have you done to achieve the desire of someone else? What have you done to give that someone else what they truly wanted? How did that affect them? And, how did that affect your everything?

We all want what we want. We all have desires for what we desire. But, if we do not, very consciously, keep all of those desire in perspective, what does that mean to the ultimate definition of your life and the life of all of those you love, live with, know, or encounter?

If you do not think about all of this, you really should.

AIN'T NO CHIMNEYS IN THE PROJECTS
22/Dec/2025 02:29 PM

I was driving today and a song came on the radio, "*Ain't No Chimneys in the Projects.*" It's a song by Sharon Jones and the Dap-King. It's one of the songs that I had totally forgotten about until I heard it again. Basically, what the song is about is, how does Santa deliver his gifts when there is no chimney for him to travel down? …You know, the whole mythos of how Santa goes from house to house in his sleigh and then goes down each chimney, delivering gifts to those who were, *"Nice."*

…As you may know, The Projects are large apartment style complexes where the less fortunate tend to live. And, being an apartment building the units do not have individual chimneys.

I don't know about you, but I've never had a chimney. No matter where I've lived, I never had a fireplace where a chimney is needed. I had this friend, way back in the way back when, he rented this house for a time with his girlfriend and they had a chimney. Every now and then, when I was visiting, he would light up the fire in the fireplace. But, that was never the norm of my life. I've never fired up a fire in a fireplace.

So, as the song details, how did Santa deliver my gifts?

I'm being illustrative here; obviously.

But, as we are just a couple of days away from Christmas 2025, and this timeframe is titled, *"The Season of Giving,"* all of this stuff is probably on your mind; the giving and the getting.

I was in a Thrift Store today and I was speaking, just for a moment, with this Shop Girl I've known for a long time. I asked her, *"You all set for Christmas?"* You know… Just the small talk you make with people you kinda know. Her answer, *"I don't celebrate Christmas. But, my aunt is throwing a tamale party and I'm all about that."* To each their own. ☺

But, back to The Season of Giving… Yeah, a lot of us don't have a chimney for Santa to travel down. Does that mean that we should get no gifts? Does that mean that we should not give gifts? I say, *"No."* I say this is The Time of Giving. And, no matter what your religious persuasion is—no matter what your philosophy is, take some time and give! Think about when you receive a gift. Doesn't that just make you feel all kinds of better? Why not make someone else feel that way? Give them a gift! Even if you don't personally know someone, give them a gift! It just makes everything a little bit better. And, making things better, making someone's life just a little bit better, isn't that something that we all want to do? GIVE!

THE DOGGY PARK
17/Dec/2025 05:08 PM

I think everyone understands what a Doggy Park is. A place where people bring their dogs, where they can run around, and play, (or fight), with other dogs. Most of the time it's a great experiment in allowing a dog to be a dog and have some fun with other animals of the same breed.

Think about this for a moment, however. Particularly think about this if you have a dog in your life… How much time do you spend truly thinking about what your dog wants to do?

For example, I have this neighbor who has an Alaskan Malamute. Beautiful animal. But, they never take it outside. They never let it run free. They keep in inside almost all of the time. Undoubtedly, they are destroying the essence of that living being. A large animal needs the time to be out in the air and run free.

This is just one example.

Think about yourself. What is it that you like to do? How much of your time do you spending doing what you want to do? For most/for many they do what they truly want to do as much as possible throughout their life. But, for an animal like a dog, they are completely under the control of their owner.

Let me sidestep here; just for a moment. I really hate all of these words like animal and owner, and I never use the world, *"Pet,"* unless I have to. As far as this piece goes, I'm just using them as a descriptive mechanism. Because I believe these so called, *"Animals,"* are living feeling beings, that have all of the rights that we humans possess. Yet, we control them.

And, this is the point to all of this, how much control do you hold over your furry friend? Do you care enough to take the time to come to understand what brings them joy and how much time do you spend truly trying to provide them with what brings them happiness?

If some other entity is in your life, be it a person or a so called animal, isn't it your duty to provide that life with as much happiness as possible, allowing them to do the things that brings them fun and joy?

So, if you have/if you bring any other living entity into your life, stop seeing them simply as an extension of your wants and your desires. Allow them to live what they wish to live. Stop being selfish!

KEEPING THINGS MOVING ALONG

16/Dec/2025 05:01 PM

I always try to keep things moving along. Not to hoard, but to keep the energy moving. For if you don't, then your energy gets all stagnant and stuff, and it really holds back your creativity.

Anyway, I came upon this suitcase. Well, it's more like an over the shoulder duffle. A little bit bigger than a duffle though…

I got it back in the '80s. I remember I took it with me, used it for my clothing, on my first visit to Tibet. That was a long-long time ago.

For some reason, I held onto it. Why? I really don't know. I just did. All my other suitcases from that era are long gone.

I found it in the bottom of another larger duffle. One that I keep similar style suitcases and backpacks in. The ones I use.

Anyway, I decided it was time to move it along. …All these years later. Sure, I have sentimentality attached to it. But, it's not serving its purpose. It's just sitting in the bottom of another suitcase.

On it, it still has the tags from the last flight I took with it: HKG, Hong Kong. And, Cathay Pacific Airlines.

I put it over by the front door on the flour, so I would remember to put it in my trunk so I could donate it the next time I went to a thrift store. Something happened, however. The moment I placed it there, one of my cats took up residence on it. Every day and every night, more times than not, that is where he is hanging out and sleeping. Each evening, he does a beat-it-up session on it. Clawing and making noises. He loves it! Why? I have no idea??? But, I can't just go and donate it now. He's made it his home.

I guess that's the thing about life and Life Stuff. You get it, however you get it. You use it, however you use it.

Then, you use it no more. But, just because you're done with it, that doesn't mean someone else would not love it.

Now, I have a new piece of furniture. A suitcase from the '80s, sitting over there by my front door.

Sure, I could donate it. But, I doubt that anyone would use it and love it like my cat is doing.

* * *

15/Dec/2025 02:06 PM

You can't fail if you hold no desire for success.

*   *   *

12/Dec/2025 01:01 PM

Are you complaining or are you rearranging.

* * *

12/Dec/2025 01:00 PM

What are you doing about the thing that you've done wrong?

What are you doing about the things that you've done wrong and you do not understand or believe any wrong was done?

DO YOU TAKE CASH?

11/Dec/2025 09:46 AM

I had kind of a curious experience the other day. I was in a shop and a woman walked up to the cash register and wanted to buy something and she asked the shop person, *"Do you take cash?"* Wow, I thought. Times have changed. Changed, as times always do.

I mean, when you're at street fairs or flea markets, and stuff like that, a lot of people want to only get paid via apps like Venmo or Zelle and the like. But, a store? That was strange.

I mean, I haven't carried any cash in a long time. All you need is your phone. But, I still know cash exists. I still know it is accepted at most establishments. I guess this is a sign of what is to come. Times are changing.

It's kind of like I have watched as the guitar marketplace has changed. As a longtime player, lover of, and a collector of guitars; once upon a time you never wanted any damage to befall your instrument. If you bumped it or dropped it, or whatevered it, and it got damaged, you were really upset. I used watch as people who got the smallest nick to their guitars bring it to my friend, who is a guitar luthier, and they would want him to repair it; bring it back to the way it once was.

I don't know exactly when it was, maybe about ten years ago or so, but all of a sudden that changed. It was cool to have a totally messed up guitar. So much so, that companies began to issue what they called, *"Relics."* Meaning, they made guitars that looked like they had totally been put through the wringer.

At least in my mind, it's one thing if you bought a guitar new and through the years you played it so much that it came to that level. But, to buy it like that. That just seems disingenuous.

You know, and that's the thing, times change. Reality changes. What is or is not desired changes

It's like, I was at a Target yesterday. A woman walks up to me. A woman of Roma descent. She had a baby in her arms and a shopping cart full of baby and other stuff. She said, *"Excuse me, sir. Can you buy this for me—for my baby."* Wow, that's a first. I mean, at least here in L.A., it's not uncommon to see Roma women with children begging for money outside of the Post Office and stuff. But, this was the first time I got hit up in a store. The method is constantly evolving.

It's kind of like; I've been recently having this realization. It kind of happened a little while back. I would go into a store or someplace and I would be paying the cashier or whomever. Looking at them, they are female and aging. At first glance, I would notice their age; elderly. But, look at bit deeper, and you could/can see that once upon a time they were undoubtedly an attractive young female. Probably, full of life, with all of the dreams of tomorrow that all young people hold. Now, older. All most people see is an elderly person.

That's the thing about life, it all is always changing. Sometimes things stay the same for a long period of time. Certainly, the older an individual gets, the more they want to hold onto the what once was. But, everything moves, everything changes, everything evolves.

Keep moving. Or, stay stagnant. Your choice. But, no matter how much you hold onto the what once was, it is guaranteed that it will not be that way tomorrow.

YOUR VISION VERSES YOUR REALITY

09/Dec/2025 08:37 AM

When I speak with filmmakers, or when I am leading a class on filmmaking, I am often confronted with the reality that the budding filmmaker has a vision for what they wish to their film to become, but when they are hit over the head with the reality of the reality that their film is not going to come out anywhere near what they imagined, they are quite disappointed and often times never complete their project. As a person who has been in the filmmaking game for more than a lot of years now, then as now, I always warn, particularly actors, to not expect too much from a young or new filmmaker as there is a very good chance that the film they signed up for will never be finished.

This case study has gone on since I got into the game. Way back when, when shooting on actual film was the name of the game. Moving onto video and now digital. Many people, namely the filmmaker, has a cinematic vision, and they hope to bring that vision to life, but the reality of the reality is, unless you have a very large budget then it is very-very hard to actualize. Even with unlimited budgets, it is not easy.

Certainly, in the no to low budget indie game, this is much more commonly the truth. The truth, because there are no overreaching contracts that have been signed stating the film will be competed or else. I have known so many people who hoped to bring up a film, maybe even began to shoot some scenes for it, but never finished it due to their vision not being met and/or a whole long list of other factors.

I guess I was blessed, or maybe it was and is just my mindset, but I have always accepted the reality of the fact that you must let everything simply be what it is and not try to force your unrealistic vision upon it. For if you do, your project, whatever that project that may be, will not only never meet your expectation but may never, in fact, ever be completed.

What am I saying here? Many people have an idea about what they wish to do with their life. Many people want to create that Some Thing. But, in doing this, if you are not realistic about your own limitations, if you are not willing to accept the final result, as far as that result may be from what you had initially envisioned, then, in your life, you will most probably never complete or finalize anything.

This is just some food for thought and something that you should keep in mind.

RADIO PLAYS

07/Dec/2025 08:31 AM

You know, when you hear a song being played on the radio, don't you always think that the artist who created that song is getting paid? I guess that's not always the case. I know it hasn't been the case with me more than a couple of times.

Every month, I'm emailed the breakdown of where my music is begin downloaded, played, etc. If you remember, I've made jokes about this kind of stuff in the past, sometimes on this blog, about like how I have this one song that has been played over twenty-five million times, and I've received all of like ten dollars U.S. for all those plays. I mean, come on…

In the monthly list I get, I've noticed that this one song that I created has, over the past year or so, been played tons of times by radio stations in Indonesia. Yes, several stations. It looks like they play it a lot. Money? As far as I can chart, I've received none.

I know it's long been charted how there's a disconnect between the creator and the sources that use and/or distribute music and other creative venues on the internet. I mean, it's long been understood that the consumer gets it for free, feels all good about their receiving it for free, but the creator gets nada. As someone on the creative side of that equation, I've always felt the hit about that situation. Do you, the consumer, ever even think or care about that?

But, radio… That all seems so analogue. That all seems so twentieth centuries. But still and all, they're not paying. Shouldn't they have to???

Now I, obviously, don't live in Indonesia. Though I have been there a few times. And, I think that it's great that the people there are being exposed to the music I created, and, (I guess), are liking it. And, I'm sure those radio stations are making money and paying their staff and stuff or they would not be in business. But, what about the artist? What about the composer who created the music they are broadcasting out to the ears of their listeners? Shouldn't they be paid too?

I'm sure most of you out there could care less about what I'm saying here. You've got your own life business going on, so why should you care? And, when you listen to music or watch movies or funny cat videos on Insta or YouTube do you ever even consider what the creator did/went through to create what they created? Probably not. You just consume. And, that's life, I guess. But, if a creator is not compensated, if they are not appreciated, if they are not credited, if they are not paid, then what will this world be left with?

THE EVOLUTION OF MY SINS

05/Dec/2025 03:23 PM

It's kind of funny, I guess… But, as I've written so much stuff and every now and then I will be looking for a piece I wrote for research or otherwise, for whatever reason there may be, and I come upon a some sort of something else I wrote. That was the case with what happened the other day. I came upon this chapter that ended up in one of my novels.

Sometimes I'm called to read what I came upon, most of the time I'm not. It's just a reminder of a time gone past. But, for this piece, I decide to open it up. It was an interesting read, written in a style that, (I guess), I would call my, *"Mature,"* writing style.

To subtext here…

Most people do not read poetry. Few people read novels. I guess that is to say unless it is a highly-publicized novel by a celebrated writer. Sure, in school, particularly in writing classes at the university level, students are forced to read the works of poets and novelists. But, even then, those reading assignments are mostly focused on the very well-known authors.

I believe there was a time when poetry and freedom in writing was more celebrated. Then, with changing times, leading to changing mindsets, and the internet, (of course), a lot of that changed. I mean really, when was the last time you read a book of poetry by a little-known poet or a novel by an unpublicized author?

But, back to the storyline…

I know for me, I initially wrote poetry and then later short stories and later novels from a very young point in my life. But, who reads them? I've watching, via my own personal experience, how times have changed. No one seems to be seeking out the literary works of obscure authors anymore.

I mean, there used to be bookstores where these works could be found. They were even featured! In fact, there used to be bookstores devoted to unique writings by unique authors. Now, bookstores are all but nonexistent.

I used to write that kind of stuff a lot. The stuff like that chapter from one of my novels. I thought it would/may equal something. Now, I question that.

It's like, I even was the editor of poetry magazine for a time. …Way back in the way back when. We would get tons and tons of submissions. There were a bunch of magazines like that at the time. Some of the writings were very good. Others, were terrible. The funny thing was, and one of the main reasons I quit doing that was, the moment we rejected someone, many of them would go ballistic. They believed they were the greatest poet of all time, and everyone should realize that. I cannot tell you how many treats I received based on rejecting someone's poetry. It's a strange world…

For me, I used to write what, (I guess), is called literary fiction a lot. I wrote poetry all the time. It was probably a supply and demand thing, but I stopped the fiction a long time ago, and the poetry has geared way back. There just doesn't seem like much of a point anymore. I write about other stuff now. Like this, writing about writing.

Anyway, all this being said, I believe things like poetry and short stories and novels provide a truly unique look into the mind and the mindset of the author. This is particularly the case for authors like myself who write from an autobiographical perspective.

For me, it was fun/funny to read that chapter from that book. It reminded me of the person I used to be. I don't know that people ever really change. But, I do know that, if they care to, they can truly evolve. Interesting to view who I was then and how and why I would write what I wrote.

So… You probably don't read poetry or novels or any of that kind of stuff. I'm sure your world is way too busy for any of that. But, if you want to look deeply into a person's psyche, and maybe see how they were created, and what made them the person they became, I believe that by reading such forms of literature, you may be provided with a looking glass into their soul.

* * *

02/Dec/2025 01:01 PM

If you have a drawer, you will always find something to put in it.

ABILITY VERSES TALENT

01/Dec/2025 11:40 AM

I have been a musician for virtually all of my life. I first begin training in classical guitar when I was six years old. Though I was messing around with a guitar prior to that point in time. From there, I spread out to many other instruments. In other words, I've been doing this a long time.

As I have been doing this for a long time, I've spent much of my life interacting with musicians. Particularly in the 1980s and into the 1990s, a large portion of my friend-base were musicians. So, I was constantly around music and the players who played it. Some were very-very good.

The thing that I recognized, even back then, was that there were some players who could mimic the playing of other musicians. Particularly with guitar, I knew several people who would play note-for-note that great passage or that killer lead. The thing was, though they possessed great ability and they could hit every note just as it was played on the record album, they were not great at creating their own style or their own sound or their own vibe. Thus, I realized, ability is different from talent.

What is the difference? A person with ability can imitate what other people have created. A person with talent creates their own sound.

Now, this ideology is not limited to music. It really spreads out across all spectrums.

As a martial artist, I have witnessed this, as well. There are those who can do the techniques they were taught with pure excellence. They look great! But, for many of them, there is an essence that is missing, as the practitioner is only emulating what they were taught, but not possessing an individualized personal mastery or innovation. They are not creating anything new or revolutionary in their movements.

Please keep in mind, I am not insulting anyone with what I am saying here. I am just stating a fact that few people ever consider. There are those who are at the crux of unique and personal, and possibly even revolutionary creation, and then there are those who can imitate that creation. Yet, they create nothing uniquely their own.

There are those individuals with ability verses those with talent. Then, there are all the other people who discuss the ability and the talent of others. They talk about what the person with ability can do, and what the individual with talent has created.

This is where much of the world's population finds themselves. You hear it and read it all the time. People speaking about those with ability and talent. As they have neither, they discuss those who do.

Question: Where do you find yourself in this equation? Think about it.

WHEN YOU FORGET THAT YOU DISLIKE SOMEBODY

01/Dec/2025 07:45 AM

How many people do you associate with that you do not really like? How many people do you spend time with simple because they serve a purpose in your life or that you must keep them around for any number of reasons?

I think in life, don't we all think and believe that we should only associate with people that we like? Yet, take a few steps through the pathway of life and we all end up spending time with people who do not fit that criteria. People that we may not even like particularly, but we must keep them in our life?

For me, I know, there have been several people that have come to be a part of my life that I would often question, why are they here? Of course, there are many reasons and answers to that question, yet I allowed them to be here. Why?

Of course, there are situations like school or jobs or ??? where you must keep someone in your life that you do not really like. That's just life, I guess? But then there are those others that are there because you allow them to be there but deep down inside you wish that was not the case.

I think that when you are young. …Young, prior to adulthood, the choice(s) of who you willingly allow into your life is easier. You like them, they are there. You don't like them, they are gone. But, there are always a million variables in that conclusion and that decision.

Like I always say, life is defined by availability. Whereby, at least in this case, you can only choose from who you can choose from.

Then, there is the other side of this issue. People that pursue you and pursue being a part of your life even though you constantly try to shew them away. I know in my life, I have experienced many examples of that.

Just like you pursuing someone—you trying to be a part of someone else's life… Why you do that is all in your own mind. It is in your mind, but it may not be in theirs.

I guess what this all comes down to is, though you may wish for your life to be a certain way—though you may wish for it to be populated with a certain group of people, that may not turn out the way that you desire. And, if your pursuit of being in the life of those who don't really want you there, what have you accomplished?

Life, and associations, and interactions, it is always a complicated subject. Complicated, particularly on the interpersonal level. I know I always try to be nice to everyone. I know I always try to be accepting of everyone. I know I aways try to be understanding of everyone and their life motivations. But, at the end of the day, that mindset has, in many cases, hurt me more than it helped me.

So, this is all just a, *'Keep it in mind,'* sort of idea.

Who are you with? Why are you with them? Or maybe better put, why are they with you?

Think about it. Be honest with yourself. You may be surprised at the answer.

THE WHO THAT THEY NEVER KNEW

29/Nov/2025 04:54 AM

I watched this movie last night. It was a Rom Com or as I like to call them a, *"Ro Co."* It was more up to my lady's speed. ...Did it for her. But, it told the story of how this one girl and guy go for a romantic getaway weekend and the girl had all of these ideas that they were locked up in love but the guy just saw them as a situation in the now. It all unfolded from there.

Basically, it was telling the story of how people never really know one another.

If you step back in time a bit, back to the year 2000, the musical artist Pete Yorn released a music video for his great song, *Strange Condition.* In it, his face is totally blurred whenever anyone is looking at him. Meaning, no one really sees who he truly is.

I had a very strange experience two days back, on Thanksgiving. We go over to the house of my wife's cousin, where the family's Thanksgiving festivities are generally held. The guy is a great host! I could never do what he does. Much of her family were there.

Now, I have known the adults in this group for the better part of forty years. Some I met when they were teenagers. They grew up, got married, had children, some got divorced, got married again. Some of the children are now deep into adulthood and living their own life. The point being, I have known these people forever.

The family talk got going, as it tends to do at these functions, and one man mentions my book on Hapkido. *"You wrote a book,"* comes the exclamation expression from the mouth of one of the family members. Like she was in total disbelief. Then another, and then another. I was dumbfounded. I have associated with these people forever, and I realized that at least some of them know absolutely nothing about me. The guy had a copy of the book. The one daughter, who is now in her late twenties, grabs it in awh.

"Do you how many books I've written," was the only thing I could think to say.

These people don't know me at all! And, they are supposed to be my family.

I realized that nobody knows anything about anybody unless they want to. That they are so locked up in their own life that most do not even care.

Now I get it. I am a bit of a reserved person, and I certainly never go out singing my own praises. But, to not know something as elemental as that about me. I mean, come on…

I've spoken about this a lot in this blog and elsewhere, but whenever you create something, whenever you step into the realm of public attention, people make up conclusions about you. They think they know who and what you are and why you do what you do. But, they are so often wrong in their conclusions. Yet, their conclusions, they broadcast to the world. That's why I've never like sites like Wikipedia. I mean sure, I use it periodically myself to find out information. But, sites like that are so biased. If a person has one fan or a lot of fans, they can completely shift the context of the article. That's the same if a person has haters. I mean, how is there any truth in that kind of dissemination of information?

It's like with my films, particularly since I've uploaded many of them to YouTube, I get hit with a lot of questions. And, that's fine. But, these people don't even try to do their own research. I mean, for many of the films I have a page on my site where that question was answered a million years ago. But, I guess it comes down to, why bother trying to do your own research?

What I am saying here is… Or, many better put, questioning, what do truly know about anybody? Really? Do you try to truly know and understand that individual or do you simply wish to project your own appraisal of their life and their life works?

Ask yourself, who do you truly know?

Ask yourself, who truly knows who and what you actually are?

* * *

26/Nov/2025 01:24 PM

Every time someone is crying, someone else is laughing.

THINKING ABOUT YOUR EGO

25/Nov/2025 01:34 PM

For people who do not walk the spiritual path, they never even think about their ego. They never even question why they are trying to look good, be smarter, know more, make more money, or become more respected than someone else. All they do is to do what they do, trying to be the most that they can be.

On the spiritual path, however, this mindset is highly looked down upon. One is taught not to put their ego first. To keep it in check. In fact, they are schooled in the ideology that doing things with ego as the basis is, in fact, wrong; not good.

Right now, think about your own life. How much time do you spend getting dressed in the morning; choosing just the right clothing so you will look the way you want to look? How much time do you spend working with your hair? How much time do you spend putting on your makeup? And, so forth.

But, even more than that, how much time do you spend thinking that you know something that someone else does not known? That you are somehow more knowledgeable than someone else? That you are somehow right, when someone else is wrong? That you are better, based in whatever ideology that you hold—better than someone else?

You see, ego is a very sublet element of life. It is a subject that few people dive into. They are simply driven by the desire to be better, prettier, smarter, richer, more loved, and/or more. How about you? How much did do you spend checking your ego? How much time do you spend holding yourself back, to keep yourself from doing ego-based things? For most, it is never.

Have you ever done something like put on a piece of clothing and think that you look really good wearing it? But then, maybe you spill something on it, and it has a big stain. Have you ever perhaps wore a style of clothing that you think makes you look really cool wearing it, but then people make fun of you? All of this and more is a byproduct of you basing your life on your ego.

Truly, how often do you ask yourself the question, *"Is what I am doing based in ego or is it based in a sense of purity?"*

What it really comes down to is, what are you doing and why are you doing it? Can you be honest enough with yourself to answer that question truthfully?

Do you want to be a better person? Do you want to be a more spiritual person? Do you want to make this world a better place-based from your position in it? If you do, the first thing you need to do, is to check your ego and stop yourself from doing anything based in your ego. Can you do that?

CAT'S IN THE CRADLE

24/Nov/2025 08:20 AM

I don't know about you, but I get some fun cat videos popping into my feed. I guess that's because I like cats, and, of course, all other animals. But, because I've had cat orientated furry friends in my life for the better part of the past forty years, well…

Anyway, every now and then, I get the lists of and about cats coming up in my feed. In this one, (and others), they state that one of the facts of having a cat in your life is that you will never get a full night's sleep. …As a cat will always bother you. How true!

But, is that really a bad thing?

I mean, each of the cats that have been a part of my life have had such a unique personality. They are each so different. One cat we had would plant himself on our pillow every night. If I ever woke up and looked at him, he was totally awake. The cat psychologists say, that he was protecting us, keeping watch over us, so there could be no attack. Thanks!

I know some people lock their cats out of their bedroom at night, just so they can get a good night's sleep. But again, the cat psychologists say, that behaving in that manner really hurts the feelings of your cat. And, I believe that. I have watched and cats possess every single emotion that humans do. They just present somewhat differently. Some people, even put their cats in cage. How wrong is that!!!

My two current cats, are quite the waker-upers. One, he comes in at least once a night and does a whole kneading session on the covers. Wake up! The other one is a total cuddler. A total bed hog. She comes in and plants herself right up against my back when I go to bed. From there, all night long, every time I turn over, she snuggles in, so by the end of the night I am just hanging on the edge of the bed.

The thing is, this is life. This is living life. This is interactive life. This is truly living. Something that I believe many people do not do. All they want is control. All they desire is power. All they want is what they want. They do not want to give—give in.

Now, you don't have to interact with cats to truly live and come to understanding humanity and life and all of that good stuff. It can come to you defined by how ever you want it to be defined. But, at least from my perspective, you must live, you must interact, you must care for something—care for them more than you for yourself. Because if you don't, what does that leave with you?

Is getting a good night's sleep really more important than having some being/someone caring about you and loving you?

BLOOD IS THICKER THAN WATER

23/Nov/2025 07:30 AM

I believe as we come into the holiday season it is an interesting and even insightful time to look at the interrelationships between people. In many ways, this is a hard subject to explore as it is so rooted in personal belief and a projection of understanding. Though it may be rooted in personal belief and projected understanding, in all of this, there is also a denial of what is actually taking place.

For example, let's focus on the family for a moment. Think about your own family. Think about your own interrelationship with your family. If you view it with an open mind, I believe you will see that those who truly make up your family, those who possess the same bloodline as yourself, are those who are always held the closest. Meaning, even if you have an issue with them, and you may not even like them all the time, they are the ones who remain a constant in your life, and you will always allow them a space in your mind and your heart.

If you turn this thought process around to what may be defined as your friends, think about how many so-called friends have come and gone in your life, throughout time. I would imagine that many people, people that you one time defined as a friend, have come and gone, in and out of your life, but those people who are truly your family, those you have a blood tie with have remained. Remained, for better or for worse.

In this truth, I believe that we can each see a trend that constitutes the definition of what a family truly is, and how our interrelationships are truly defined.

I know from own perspective, I have been confronted with this truth many times ever since I was very young.

Let me tell you a kind of funny story here… Funny, in that not so funny sort of way… But, it does provide insight to what I'm speaking about.

Okay, let's step back a million years. My long-time friend finds a woman. She gets pregnant. They decide to get married. I'm the only person who went along with them to Vegas as their witness. They have their baby. All-good. It's time for her to be baptized. He asks me to be the godfather. Sure. But, as they are Catholic, he tells me I have lie to the priest and tell him that I'm Catholic, as well. I guess you have to be of the same faith to be a godfather in that sect of the religion??? I'm probably going to hell over that one. Anyway… But, I happily did it. Did it for a friend and all. She's baptized. I'm the godfather. Whenever it's Christmas time, they always ask good ole Uncle Scott to buy the most expensive gift for her. Sure. Whatever… Happy to do it. Time passes; I rarely see the guy as he works in Vegas all week and only comes home to L.A. on the weekends. More time passes, his daughter gets married. I'm not even invited to the wedding. She has a kid, never told me anything about it. It wasn't until my friend's funeral that I even knew anything about any of it. But, the blood all did.

You see, blood is everything.

And, if you've been read this blog for a while, you know I've discussed similar situations in association with my marrying into a Korean family. As a white guy, I'm there, but I'm not. I'm always on the outside. Plus, I've told other stories, about other situations, in various places, that all lead to a similar conclusion.

My point being, if you have a blood tie to someone, there is always that connection. If you don't, you don't. It's as simple as that.

Think about all of the friends you had, once upon a time, and then you had them no more. Think of all the loves you had, that you thought would last forever, but they are long gone.

As the old saying goes, blood is thicker than water. It's important to keep that in mind.

*   *   *

23/Nov/2025 06:12 AM

There can be a problem with everything if you look for a problem in anything.

There can be a blessing with everything if you look for a blessing in anything.

ART HAS CHANGED

18/Nov/2025 05:42 PM

I was popping around through some old files today and I came upon the manuscript for one of my novels. I opened it up, just to have a glance, and I came upon this one passage where I was discussing how I had been painting…

Back when I wrote that novel, I lived in this flat in Hermosa Beach with a gigantic kitchen. I was really into painting big back then so I would cut a large piece of canvas off of the roll of canvas I had bought, and I would staple gun it to the wall. There, I would paint.

You know, painting takes effort. You have to buy the canvas, buy the paints, buy the brushes. Back then, I was into oil, so I also had to buy the turpentine and the thinner. …All before I could paint.

But, that was all good. It was/I felt it was all part of the process.

I would turn the music up and get to work. Late, late into the late night.

I've spoken a lot about this… About how filmmaking used to be so much more complicated. You had to buy (or rent) a camera. Buy the film. Shoot the film. Develop the film. Transfer the film. Edit the film. Sync the sound. All before you could ever even get close to a finished project. Now, all you need is your iPhone.

Music was the same. It took a lot of time effort and work to record a track. Now, it happens with a touch of button or a keyboard stroke.

I guess that's all part and parcel to what I'm saying here. Art has changed. It has become at least different, if not easier.

Art is in the moment. And, trust me, I believe that is very Zen. But, think about it… A lot of the Content Creators out there all they do is grab their phone and talk some talk into it for a moment or more. Post it. And, the art, (their art), is given birth to. They have millions of followers.

And that's the thing… Art changes. It changes with time. It changes with culture. It changes with technology. And, if you don't move with the times—if you don't change with the times—if you don't accept the change that has taken place, what does that make you?

I don't have an absolute answer for that. You may have the exact answer??? All I can say, if you don't accept the new in the art for whatever the art may be, all you are doing is remaining stagnant, locked into a time gone past.

If you don't let art be whatever the creator of that art sees their art to be, then are you evolved enough to truly understand art?

BE CAREFUL WHAT YOU WISH FOR 2

16/Nov/2025 07:57 AM

The other day I was complaining about how my hummingbird feeders had become inundated with hummingbirds and I had to keep filling them up all the time. What has happened next is a bit curious…

From what I've read, hummingbirds are a very territorial creature. They protect what they believe is theirs. And, don't get me wrong, I am no expert on hummingbirds. That's just what I read. I'm just a guy with a couple of hummingbird feeders.

Now, I had never seen this that much. Sure, the hummingbirds would chase each other around. And, some would be more aggressive than others. But, they would all eventually get their drink.

What has happened now is that two hummingbirds have come to own their individual feeder. One sits on the top of one of them, the other on top of the other. Whenever any hummingbirds try to come to drink, they chase them away. They sit there in guard mode, chasing all up-comers away. Occasionally, they take a drink, then they go back to their post. Very strange…

Kind of funny, and if you have read that blog that I wrote a couple of days ago, you may even think that/this is what I want. I have not had to fill up the feeders for a few days now. And, the sugar water has gone down very little. But, that's not what I want. Really, I want to provide sustenance for the whole community or I would just take down the feeders and throw them away.

I think we have all probably had to deal with bullies like this at some point throughout our life. I know I have. Maybe it is the big scary guy who grew up way too fast or flucked out and was held back in grammar school or junior high. Maybe it was a gang or gangs, like was the case I had to content with when I was young. Maybe it was someone on the internet hiding behind their keyboard and screen. Maybe it was a lawyer. Maybe it was a boss. Maybe it was a??? Whatever or whomever the case, I believe most of us have had to deal with a bully at some point in our life. And, if you have, you know that it is fucked up. It leaves you with a very bad feeling inside.

But, what can you do in those situations? I think there is no real answer. I mean, life is not like a Bruce Lee movie where you are attacked by a swam of people and you kick all of their asses and emerge victorious. Or, a place where Right always overcomes Wrong. To get past whatever bully situation you find yourself in, you just gotta play it by ear.

The fact of the fact is, a lot of life is like that. There is someone on top, keeping you from getting where you want to be, (to get your drink of sugar water), and no matter how hard you try, they just keep you from getting or becoming.

Maybe, and this is just a big maybe, the best path forward is to not try to fight at all. Leave, go somewhere else where the free drink is way more available and not patrolled by a bully with wings.

*   *   *

16/Nov/2025 07:31 AM

A dream is nothing more than a fantasy that you have no control over.

THE PROJECTION OF WHO YOU ARE

14/Nov/2025 02:13 PM

I have long said you can always tell someone who has money. Even if the clothing they are wearing is very shabby, they will always be wearing expensive shoes and an expensive watch.

For the most part, though times and trends have changed, that statement holds true. The subtle elements of how a person presents themselves is the telltale sign of who and what they truly are.

How do you present yourself? Are you consistent in the presentation you present to the world? Or, do you vacillate between one thing and another?

Some people base all that they wear in a sense of ego. Maybe that is presented by wearing only designer clothing, expensive jewelry, and the like. Maybe it is just the opposite. The person only wants to be observed as down, so they wear cheap everything. Maybe someone is locked into a very expressive mode of style, so they only wear clothing that depicts that genre. Whatever the case, if a person holds true to the way they view themselves on the inside—the inside to the outside, they allow anyone who encounters them to gain at least a partial understanding of who they believe themselves to be.

So, again… How do you present yourself to world? And, perhaps most importantly, do you hold firm in your presentation?

Here's the facts, if you want to be known as a something, you must always hold tight and be consistent with the image you portray to the world around you. Of course, all that you wear, all that you do with elements like your body and your hair are based in ego-domination and ego-presentation, but, if you do not hold tight to how you view yourself on the inside, and how you present that to the world on the outside, no one can ever be sure of who or what you truly are.

THE PUFF-PIECE

13/Nov/2025 08:43 AM

The new doc on Eddie Murphy came out yesterday on Netflix. Interesting piece, I guess…

Now, don't get me wrong, I have nothing but respect for Murphy. He was and is a groundbreaking performer who deserved his rapid rise to the top and praise for all of the barriers he broke down not only for himself but for those who came after him. The doc talks about that.

Of late, I have been watching a number of documentaries presented about famous people and/or groups. Just off the top of my head there was the one on Michael J. Fox. The one about Stiller and Meara, told via the thoughts and the words of Ben Stiller. The one about Ozzy, created just after his passing. Stepping back just a bit, there was the one about Sly, Christopher Reeves, Pamela Anderson, Stallone: Frank: That Is, Devo, and…

They were all good and informative works in their own right. But, the overwhelming vibe of them is that they were Puff-Pieces. Meaning, that as truthful as the story being told may have been, they don't really dig into any of the dirt of the individual. They simply present the more positive aspects of their life.

Now, I get it… Isn't that the way we all wish to be viewed and judged, only by our positive attributes?

I believe we are living through one of the truly historic periods of American history right now. This has been highly-defined by the rise of Trump to the Presidency of the United States. Not once, but twice. Whether you love or hate him is not the issue. But, just look at all of the dirt that has been put out there about the man. From the moment he was elected president, people have gone after him in so many ways: cable-news network presentations, articles, books, impeachments, you name it… I think most people don't think about this, but think how many books have been written about the man over the past few years. Sure, all of the authors are doing it to make bank. But, that does not change the content of most of these writings. They present a very negative picture of the man. Yet, and again, he did become President of the United States twice. And, he is in office right now.

From a personal perspective, and I truly do not know why this is, but some people on the internet and elsewhere have talked shit about me, taking my words out of context, turning my philosophies upside down, and presenting all kinds of false appraisals and ideologies, about my creative works, and myself. I won't go into why I believe they have done this in this piece, because that's not really the point. …At least not for this piece. But, the fact of the fact is, they have. Why? Why would anyone focus on a negative appraisal of my life or my works in the first place? A person who has spent his entire life concentrating on the positive, trying to make the world and the lives of people a better place, and to give back, via my art and my everything else, in any small way that I can.

I think it is interesting how people place themselves in a position of judge and jury over others. Judge and jury, where, at least from my perspective, they are so wrong about so many things. Now, people could stand up for me, as I do seem to have a certain about of, *"Likers,"* out there. But, it seems that nobody wants to get their hands dirty or to go toe-to-toe. So, what does that say about them? What does that say about me? And, this all goes to the truth of the truth in the projected reality about that Some One Else.

I remember when that group of students at a Midwestern university did that multi-part pseudo bio-pic about *Zen Filmmaking* and myself. That was like fifteen years ago. Or, more??? They uploaded it to YouTube. It's still there if you feel like checking it out.

I never watched the whole thing, but the little I saw of it, the piece was pretty funny. Though the piece took a lot of swipes at *Zen Filmmaking,* DGJ, and myself, it was done from a light-hearted approach. Making it a fun piece to watch. With this, what could be viewed as a critical comment was erased by the kitschy humor.

I have no idea who the people who created that pseudo-doc were or are. I never met any of them. And, I have no idea whatever became of them. They did that piece when *Zen Filmmaking* was on the lips of everyone in the film game. So???

The reason I bring this/that piece up is because, I, and people like me, are an easy target. People who create and present their art, or their whatever, from a new and different perspective.

But, more to the point, and to the truth of the truth, do those Puff-Piece Docs present the truth? Just as do the Attack-Ads present the truth? The answer is, no.

Like, I finally got around to watching the multi-part series that was done on the WeWorks founder, Adam Neumann and his wife Rebekah Neumann, WeCrashed, played by Jared Leto and Anne Hathaway. And, probably not unlike the film, *The Disaster Artist,* created about the production of the movie, The Room and Tommy Wiseau by James Franco, the series was revealing yet factual. (Of course, with a theatrical twist). And, I think that is the key word in all of this, *"Factual."*

The thing is, though these Puff-Piece Docs I am speaking about may be truthful—truth, from one perspective, they are not fully factual as they leave out many of the details that the primary focus of the productions do not want to be spoken about.

Every now and then, like just recently, when someone asked me what would I think about someone doing a biopic about me, I always jokingly say, it has already been done, referencing that piece made by those university students years ago. But, here is the factual fact, of everything I have heard, watched, or read that was written about me, the people doing the doing get it wrong. In no case, whether the piece was based on positivity or negativity, did they get it, (me), right. They misrepresent my philosophy. They misquote my words and my writings. They misconstrue my motivations for the art I create. And, they are wrong about my process of creation of the films, writings, art, and other things I have done. So, why are they doing it? Doesn't that make everything they say or do based upon a lie? And, if this is the case, what does that say about them as a human being and what they are putting out there to the world?

And, maybe even more importantly, what does that say about the people who view what they say and believe it?

I guess what I'm saying here is, why has no one made a Puff-Piece about me??? I'm the one who created something.

I mean, even some of the people who have thrown shade my direction have used some or all of my filmmaking philosophy to create their films. I find that very disingenuous. Not to mention the A-Listers who used some or all of it in their productions. …As has been documented.

I get it, the only reason anyone talks about anyone's anything, other than their own, is because they want to make a name for themselves as a, *"Knower."* They want to either help or to hurt the person they speak about. But, in all of that, where is the truth in a person's truth? Is it found in the way they want their life ideally projected, like in the documentaries I have spoken about in this piece? Or, is it found somewhere else? Not defined by the mind of that someone else who thinks they know more about a person than the person themselves, but in the truth of the truth that can only be found in the inner-reaches of an individual's soul? Think about it…

You can lie to me. But, you can't lie to yourself.

BE CAREFUL WHAT YOU WISH FOR

12/Nov/2025 01:52 PM

Like the old saying goes, *"Be careful what you wish for."*

Back during the pandemic, when we were all under lockdown, each afternoon my lady and I would take a walk around the neighborhood. You know, to keep the energy flowing, stay in shape, and all of that kind of stuff.

We would walk by this one neighbor's place, and we noticed that they had a couple of hummingbird feeders hanging up and they had tons and tons of hummingbirds flying all around, feeding, etc. We thought how cool that would be.

Anyway, we set up a hummingbird feeder, and a few hummingbirds would pop by each day to feed. All was well with the world.

Over time, a few of our neighbors also set up hummingbird feeders. It was kind of cool to watch the hummingbirds fly from ours to theirs and theirs to ours.

Time ticks by, as a time always does, and I started to notice that none of my neighbors were refilling their hummingbird feeders. Some of them were really nice glass pieces. Pretty to look at. But, no sugar water was in them any-more…

What started to happen is that all the hummingbirds in the area begin to feed from the two feeders that are hanging on our patio. All good at first. But, then/now, it has gone crazy. Hummingbirds are feeding from them all day long. I mean constantly! So much so, that I have to refill them at least once a day.

Now, don't get me wrong, I love hummingbirds and nature and all of that kind of good stuff. But, it has gone from being fun—refiling the feeders maybe once a week, to becoming a chore.

My lady and I were discussing this last night, and our hummingbird feeding neighbor, from a time gone past, and we laughed, *"Be careful what you wish for,"* because we thought all of those hummingbirds being at that person's feeders was cool. Cool, until we faced the hard, cold reality of it.

Right now, I look out my window, and I count fifteen of them feeding. I guess I'm the only one in the area who still cares enough to care that they get feed. But, it is a chore.

Just some food for thought… *"Be careful what you wish for."*

HIGHER CONSCIOUSNESS UNWANTED

11/Nov/2025 09:25 AM

I had two conversations over the past couple of days that were kind of interesting. And, they both tied into one another.

This one individual, who, like I, has spent most of their life walking the Spiritual Path. (Spiritual Path, for lack of a better term). They were speaking about the fact that they always try to bring spirituality into all that they do and have it spread from them out to the world. Nothing wrong with that, I believe we can all agree.

What they stated next, I found interesting. They said no matter how much they try to do all things with a sense of consciousness and to be a positive influence, all of the people they interact with don't seem to get it. Whether this is at their job, when they are in the out and about, and so on. *"People don't want to be spiritual,"* they exclaimed. *"Duh,"* I said.

I was speaking with this other person who has taught the physical aspects of Yoga for a few decades by this point in time. I need to spell that out, because what most people refer to as, *"Yoga,"* is actually, Hatha Yoga, and is a very small part of the over-spanning cornucopia that Yoga truly is. But, I won't go into that here.

Anyway, they were saying how they always saw Hatha Yoga as a means to bring the body into alignment with the spirit and to help an individual transcend to the deeper realms of truth, reality, and god-consciousness. But, no matter how much they describe this in their classes, even during the meditation segments, nobody really wants to hear it. They just do Yoga for very physical reasons. I didn't say, *"Duh,"* but I thought it.

I did, however, discuss how that is something I have experienced for the better part of my life. People do not care about True Spiritually. Do you?

Now, if you ask most Westerners about their religion, their spirituality, or their beliefs, they will claim that they are a Christian. But, do they truly practice True Christianity? True Christianity, as it is laid out in the Bible? I would say, probably not.

If you ask many of the people who arise from the Middle East, what is your belief? They would claim, Islam. But, do they truly practice True Islam? True Islam, as it is laid out in the Koran? I would say, probably not.

If you ask many of the people who arise from India, what is your belief? They would claim, Hinduism. But, do they truly practice True Hinduism? True Hinduism, as it is laid out in the various Hindu Scriptures? I would say, probably not.

This is the same with those who claim Buddhism, Judaism, or any other religion or philosophy as their system of faith.

The fact is, most people do not care about Higher Consciousness or True Spirituality. And, there is nothing that you can do to make them care about it. They only care about what they care about at any given moment of time. How about you? Truly, do you care about spirituality? Do you try to live a life based upon true spirituality, however you may define that?

Sad, but true. Very few people care about living a spirituality-based life.

MAKING THE WORLD A BRIGHTER PLACE

10/Nov/2025 02:05 PM

What do you do to make the world a brighter place? Really, what do you do to make the world a brighter, happier, and more fun place? Do you do anything?

I tend to travel a lot. So, I have spent many a moment driving my car into this one specific long-term parking lot at LAX. This, when I've not decided to go Uber Black.

I've been kind weirded out on whole the Uber experience of late as the last time I took a ride with them the driver they sent me was obviously sick—sneezing and wiping his nose and all of that kind of stuff. But, what could I do??? I had already gotten into his car?

Anyway, I got sick. Obviously, from his germs. And, from this, the wife got sick. Not good! I wonder, can you sue Uber for one of their drivers making you sick?

Anyway… I always go to this one long-term lot when I'm parking my car at LAX. From there, and back to there from the airport, they have a shuttle that takes you to and fro. I've had various levels of experiences in that shuttle. But, all lost to the world of whatever…

The last time I was getting a ride back from the airport, a week or so ago, it was a totally new and unique experience, however. The driver had this great euro-dance music playing. He had actually taken the time to set up colored lights that were flashing on the ceiling of the shuttle bus. He even had a screen up in the front, showing this young woman dancing along to the music. Though the ride only lasted for a few minutes, it was great! I mean what an experience! It just made the All and the Everything of those few moments that much better.

Do you ever do anything like that? Do you ever take the time to make someone else's world, someone that you may not even know, that much better? Do you ever set about on a course of actually trying and doing and actualizing, and all of that kind of stuff, to make the world a brighter place. If you don't, maybe you should.

THE ZEN

www.ingramcontent.com/pod-product-compliance
Lightning Source LLC
LaVergne TN
LVHW010053110826
845155LV00028B/317

* 9 7 8 1 9 4 9 2 5 1 9 2 0 *